Did You Know?

KETTERING

A MISCELLANY

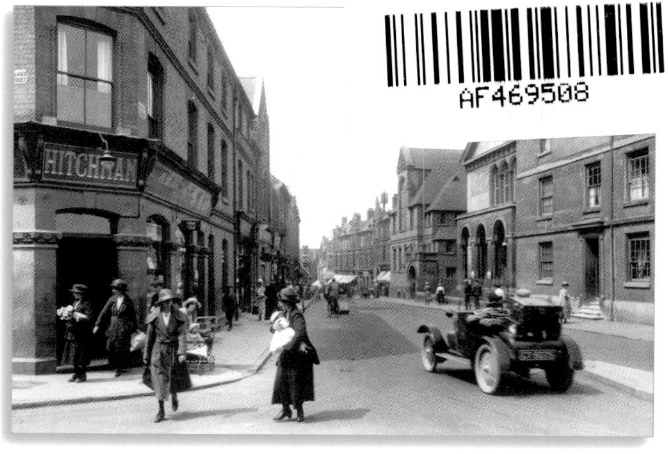

Compiled by Julia Skinner

With particular reference to the work of Malpas Pearse

THE FRANCIS FRITH COLLECTION

www.francisfrith.com

First published in the United Kingdom in 2006 by The Francis Frith Collection®

Hardback edition published in 2006 ISBN 10: 1-84589-363-8 ISBN 13: 978-1-84589-363-7

British Library Cataloguing in Publication Data

Did You Know? Kettering - A Miscellany
Compiled by Julia Skinner
With particular reference to the work of Malpas Pearse

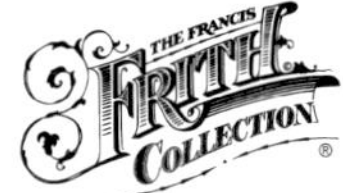

The Francis Frith Collection
Frith's Barn, Teffont,
Salisbury, Wiltshire SP3 5QP
Tel: +44 (0) 1722 716 376
Email: info@francisfrith.co.uk
www.francisfrith.com

Printed and bound in Thailand

Front Cover: **KETTERING, GOLD STREET 1922** 72230p

The colour-tinting is for illustrative purposes only, and is not intended to be historically accurate

AS WITH ANY HISTORICAL DATABASE, THE FRANCIS FRITH ARCHIVE IS CONSTANTLY BEING CORRECTED AND IMPROVED, AND THE PUBLISHERS WOULD WELCOME INFORMATION ON OMISSIONS OR INACCURACIES

CONTENTS

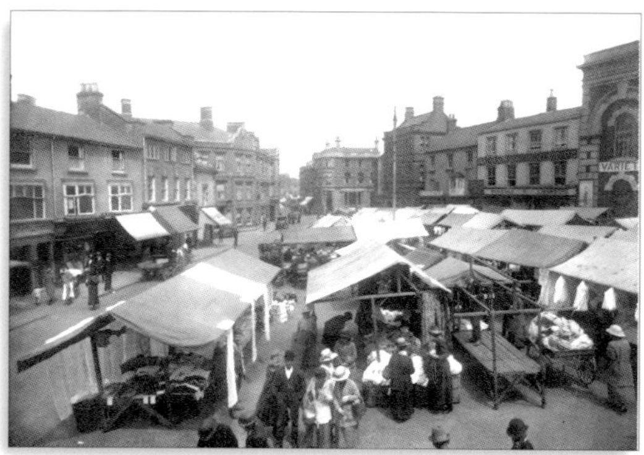

2 Introduction

4 Northamptonshire Dialect Words and Phrases

5 Haunted Kettering

6 Kettering Miscellany

43 Sporting Kettering

44 Quiz Questions

46 Recipes

48 Quiz Answers

54 Francis Frith - Pioneer Victorian Photographer

INTRODUCTION

Kettering was once a market town with a small weaving industry. From the 17th century it was a centre for the production of woollen cloth, and later of silk and plush, but even so, in 1841 42% of the population of the town and surrounding area still worked in agriculture.

By the late 19th century the Kettering area had become an important manufacturing centre for boots and shoes, specialising in heavy work boots. With the coming of the railways the town began to export footwear to the rest of the world, and Kettering grew into a web of terraced streets in clusters round factories modelled on baronial halls and Venetian palaces. The town also had a significant engineering and clothing industry, and the luxury clothing manufacturers Aquascutum built their first factory here in 1909.

As the footwear industry declined in the 20th century, Kettering diversified into more modern industries, and despite having to compete against the designated 'new town' of Corby, only 8 miles (13 km) away, Kettering has remained a prosperous town. Kettering's unemployment rate is now amongst the lowest in the UK, and the town is home to a wide range of companies, with the service and distribution sector being of particular importance to the local economy. Kettering's success is due to its good transport links, and the town also has a large and growing population of commuters because of its position on a mainline railway.

The redevelopment of the 20th century has resulted in the demolition of much of the old town centre, but the market place, a long triangle in shape, is still on the site of the first charter market, and the Kettering Heritage Quarter is well worth exploring.

Kettering's story is full of fascinating characters and events, of which this book can only provide a brief glimpse.

HIGH STREET FROM BAKEHOUSE HILL c1960 K13066

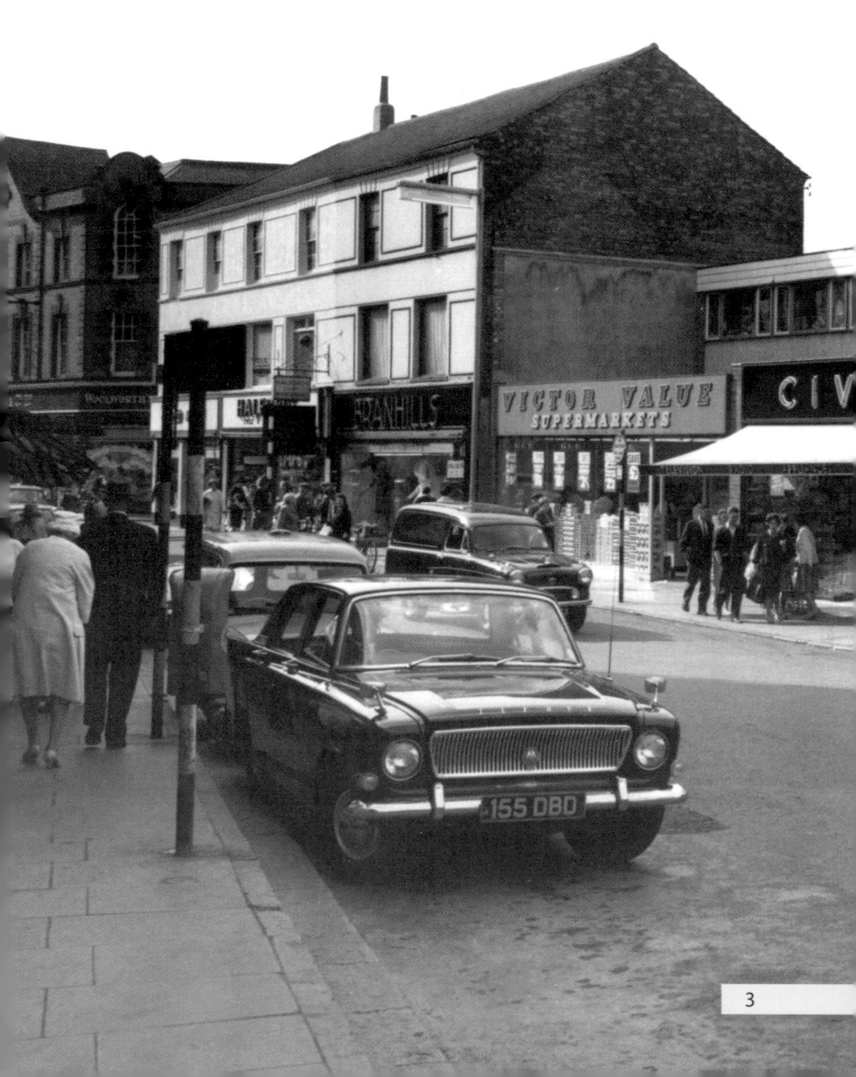

NORTHAMPTONSHIRE DIALECT WORDS AND PHRASES

'Clang' - to eat voraciously.

'Cack-handed' - left-handed, which came to mean doing something in an awkward fashion.

'Clod Hoppers' - heavy boots.

'Grandad's slippers' - mud on your boots.

'Cod Chops' - used to describe someone whose mouth is permanently open.

'Jitty' - an alley, a narrow walk way between or alongside buildings.

'Peps' - sweets.

'Me duck' - 'My dear', a term of endearment.

'Chopse' - to chat or chatter.

'Otch' - move, as in ***'Otch up!'*** - move up!

'Spotting' - starting to rain.

'Knockroad' - awkward.

HAUNTED KETTERING

The building that the Red Pepper restaurant occupies in Market Street is believed to be one of the oldest in Kettering, and not surprisingly it is linked with a ghost story.

The tale goes that in the 18th century a party of soldiers was staying in the Duke's Arms, which stood opposite where the Red Pepper building is now. With the soldiers was a young drummer boy, who became involved in an argument and was dragged outside to be murdered in an alleyway. The site of that alleyway is now the entrance to the Red Pepper, and the boy's ghost now haunts the building.

Several owners of the building in the 20th century have reported feeling uneasy in the premises and have noted strange occurrences, including mysterious noises, especially from the stock room, and sudden drops in temperature. At one time the shop assistants refused to go to the stock room alone, even though they had not been told anything about the story of the drummer boy.

In the late 20th century, whilst the building was being repaired, a dagger was found in the wall of one of the upstairs rooms, although it is not clear whether this had any link with the death of the drummer boy.

KETTERING MISCELLANY

Kettering originated in pre-Anglo-Saxon England, when it was one of a string of settlements along the Nene Valley. There is evidence of settlement in the area in the Roman period, and there was a pottery industry in the region in Roman times - kilns from this period have been found at Barton Seagrave and Boughton.

Words and names ending with 'ing' usually derive from the early Saxon word 'inga' or 'ingas', which means 'the people (or tribe) of ....' The name of Kettering in its earliest forms - Cytringan, Kyteringas and Keteiringan - therefore probably means that the area was settled by the people of a tribal leader called something like Cuthfrith or Cutfrith. However, another explanation of the place name suggests that it could derive from 'cetel', the Saxon word for a narrow valley. The town was recorded as 'Cateringe' in the Domesday Book of 1086, and by 1557 the name had become Ketteryng.

When Edward I's beloved wife Eleanor of Castile died at Harby in Nottinghamshire in 1290, the distraught king had elaborate crosses erected at the twelve places where the coffin of his 'chere reine', or 'dear queen', rested overnight on the journey from Nottinghamshire to London (this was the origin of the name of the final resting place, Charing Cross in London). Only three of these 'Eleanor Crosses' survive, and two of them are in Northamptonshire, one at Northampton and the other at Geddington, just outside Kettering; the Eleanor Cross at Geddington, at the junction of West Street and Bridge Street, is the best surviving example, and is shown in photograph 72254, opposite.

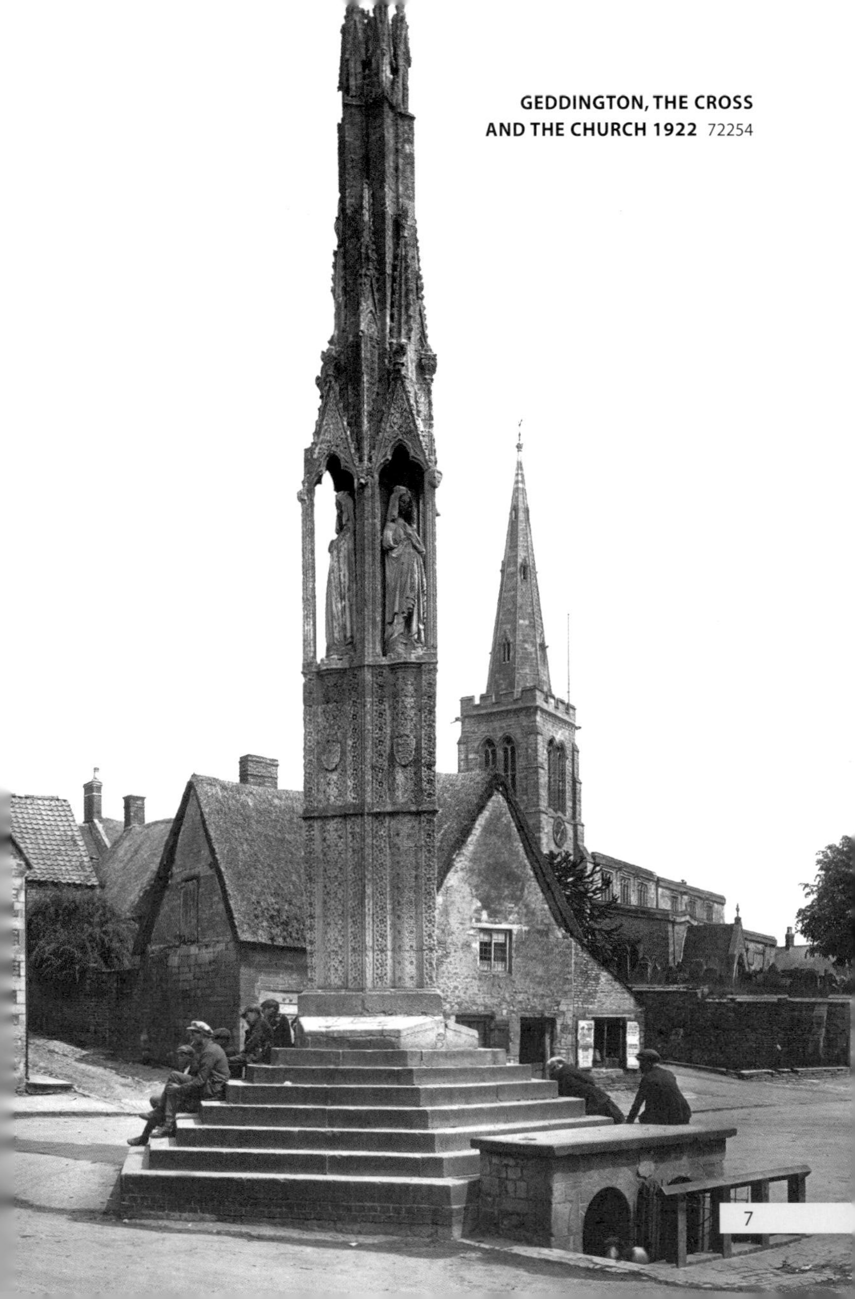

GEDDINGTON, THE CROSS AND THE CHURCH 1922 72254

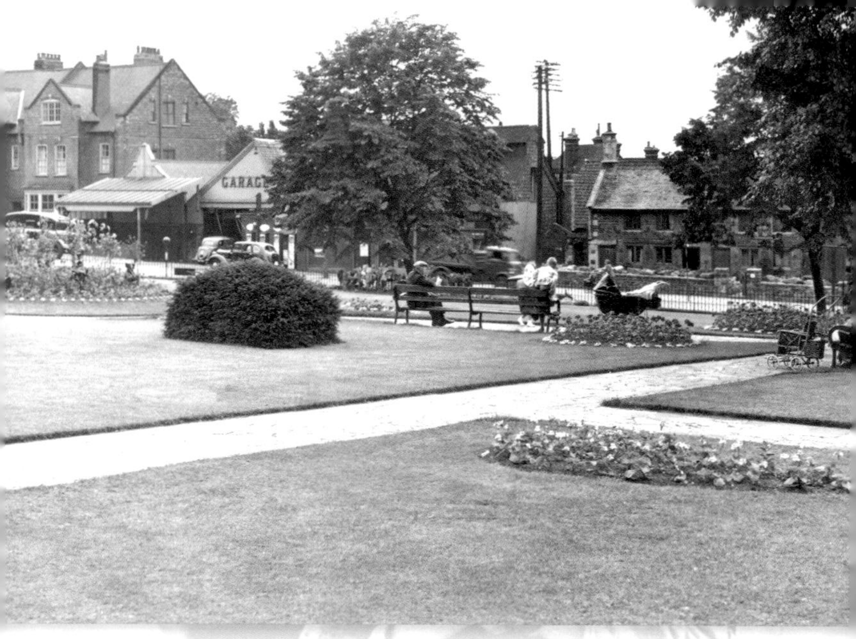

MANOR HOUSE GARDENS c1955 K13032

Photograph K13032, above, shows the busy junction at the top of Station Road and Northampton Road opposite the Manor House Gardens. The Headlands stretches off to the right. Sawyer's Almshouses can be seen through the trees to the right. Edmund Sawyer must have been a swashbuckling adventurer. He left his family home at Kettering Manor and became a merchant at Aleppo in Syria. He left £600 in 1687 for the relief of the poor in his home town, and his sister Joyce had six almshouses built with the legacy. They were turned into three dwellings in 1961.

At one time, Kettering was famous for supplying the medical profession with a particular type of stone which was ground into a powder that was used to staunch bleeding. This gave the earlier name of Staunch Lane to what is now Lower Street.

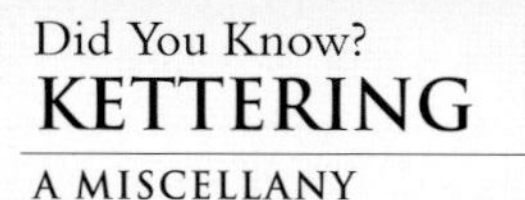

As Kettering's 19th-century manufacturers became more involved with offices in London, they built themselves homes within easy reach of the station. Large late Victorian houses lined Station Road, the adjacent Queensberry Road and The Headlands, from where businessmen could easily commute to the capital. Photograph 72236, below, shows Station Road when it was still a mainly residential area; most of the remaining houses in this road have now been turned into offices, and some have been replaced by modern flats, but in Queensberry Road and The Headlands there are still comfortable Victorian villas which are relics of Kettering's 19th-century prosperity.

STATION ROAD 1922 72236

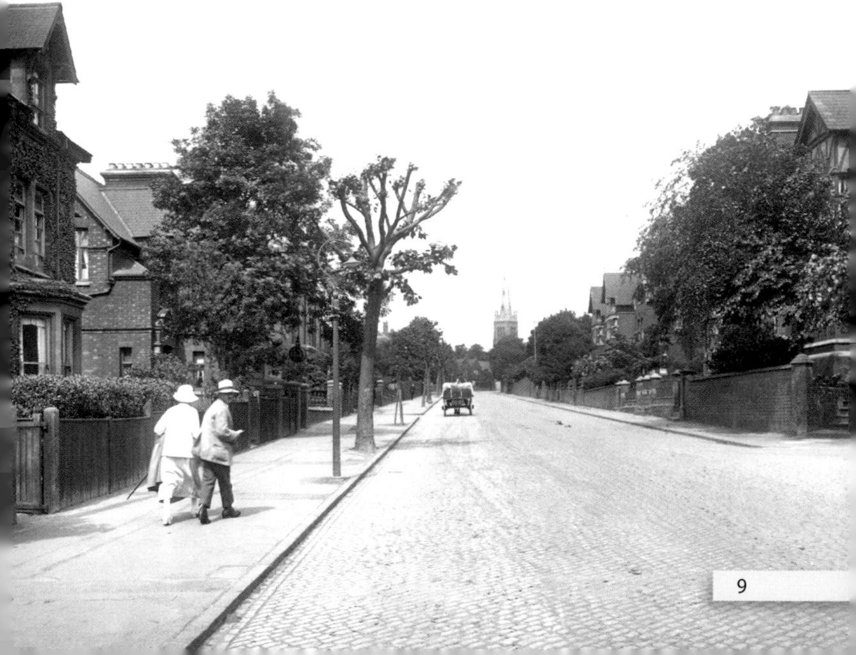

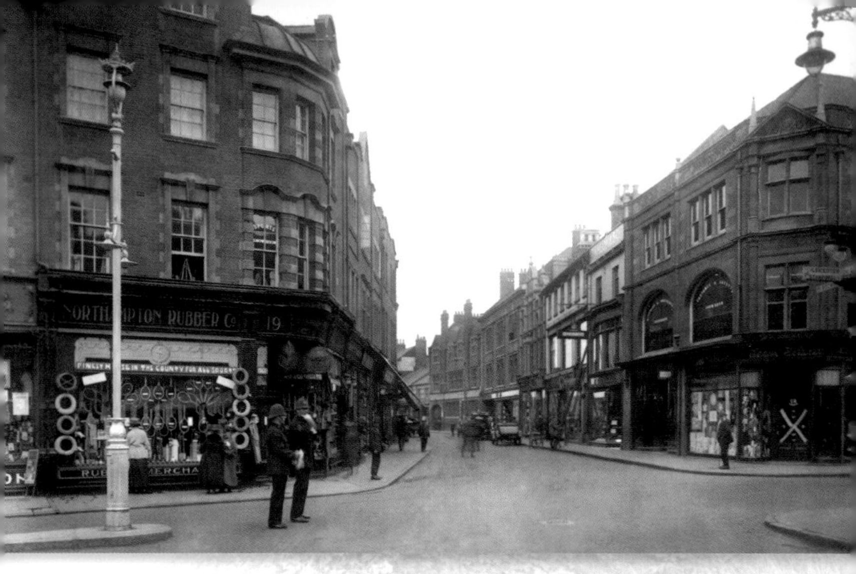

NEWLAND STREET 1922 72235

Photograph 72235 (above) shows Newland Street in 1922; on the right-hand side, on the corner of Newland Street and Montagu Street, is Ernest Woodcock's department store. This was described as Kettering's leading department store for fashions, millinery, fabrics, furnishings, furniture and household lines, and Woodcock's were also funeral directors. When you made your purchases in this store in the 1920s and 1930s the assistant put the money and bill into a brass container which was attached to a wire overhead pulley; this then went to a central cashier's office, and your change was returned the same way.

By 1227 Kettering had become large enough for Henry III to grant a charter for a weekly market on Fridays and a 'Feast' to be held for seven days in June. The markets still take place, and a fair visits the town annually. The fairground is on the edge of the Northampton Road.

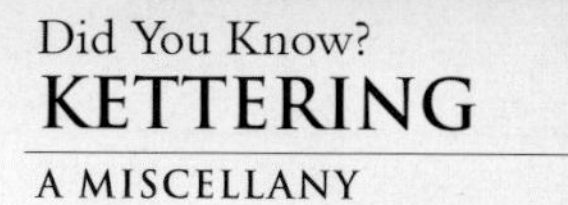

Dryland Street was originally known as Workhouse Lane, but was renamed after the town doctor who had a surgery here (and see also page 36). His neighbour was the local newspaper, the Evening Telegraph, which had offices and printing works close to the town centre for 80 years before moving to Northfield Avenue in 1976.

Photograph 72245, below, shows Northampton Road in the 1920s. This rural lane was to change dramatically in the 1930s, when it would be bordered by large detached houses with elaborate gardens. In more recent years it has become a busy road which is bisected by the A14, which links the east coast with the centre of England. The railway bridge is now too low for tall lorries, which are diverted.

NORTHAMPTON ROAD 1922 72245

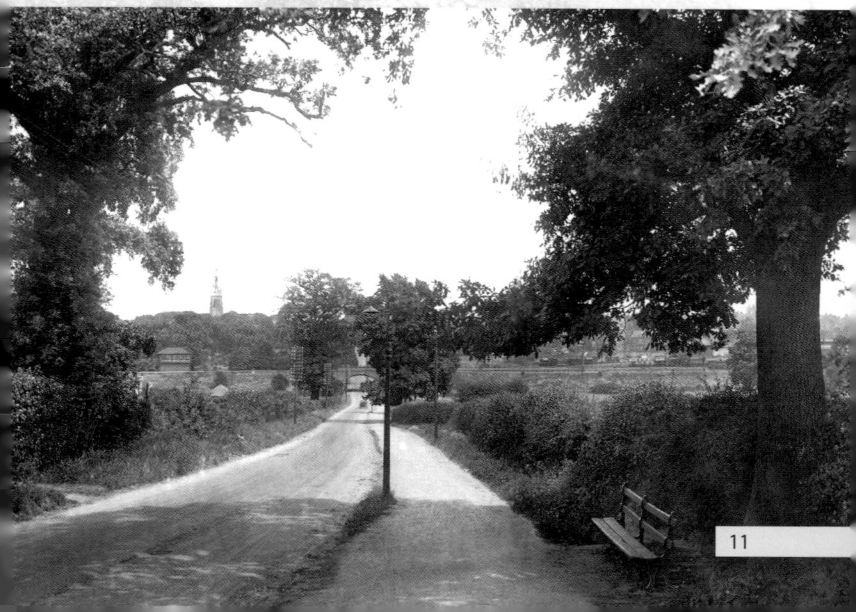

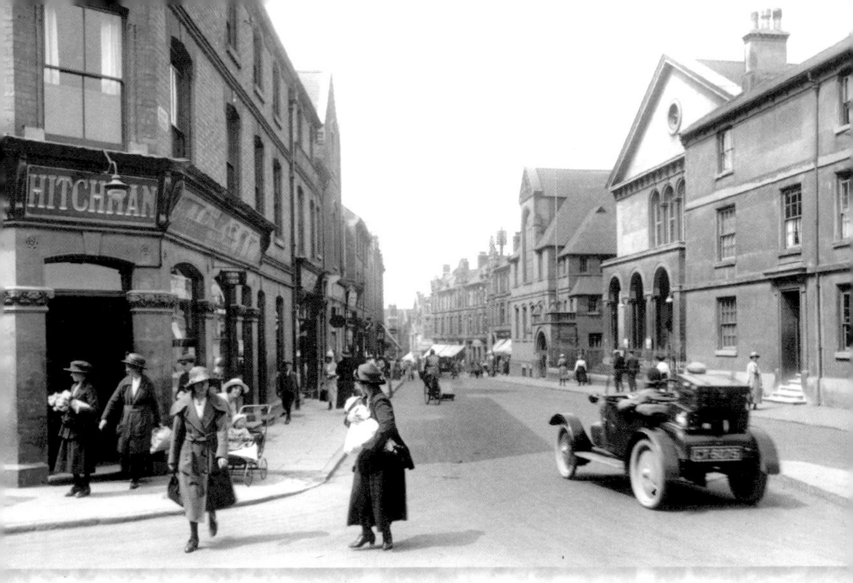

GOLD STREET 1922 72230

The gabled building seen on the right of photograph 72230, above, is the Fuller Baptist Church, which was named after Andrew Fuller, who was instrumental in founding the Baptist Missionary Society. On 2 October 1792 a group of local Baptist ministers met in Widow Wallis's house in Lower Street and formed the Baptist Missionary Society, collecting £13 2s 6d in Andrew Fuller's snuffbox to launch the movement, which disseminated medicine and education as well as religion. While Fuller stayed in Kettering and organised the Society, two missionaries from the town set out to make real changes in the world: William Carey went to India, where he translated the Bible into Bengali and founded the Agro-Horticultural Society of India in 1830, and William Knibb went to Kingston, Jamaica, where he was horrified by the realities of slavery and worked for emancipation. After imprisonment he returned to England, where he continued to campaign until the abolition of slavery in 1833. It was estimated that 300,000 slaves were liberated by his efforts. He is commemorated in Kettering in the names of Knibb Street and the Knibb Centre.

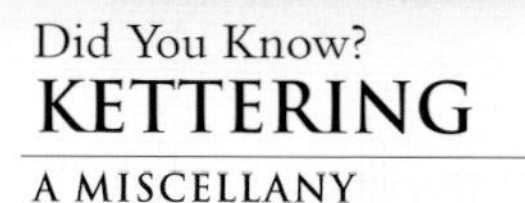

In the 10th century Kettering, then called 'Cytringan', was a gift to Aelfsige the Goldsmith from King Edwy in AD956. It is possible that Aelfsige donated the land to the Church, as a charter of King Edgar dated AD972 shows that by then 'Kyteringan' belonged to the monks of Medeshamstede, under the diocese of Peterborough. When Edgar died in AD975, powerful noblemen moved in and snatched back the lands which had been given to the Church; Leofsige grabbed Peterborough, Oundle and Kettering. The lands were reclaimed for the Church after Edward the Confessor became king in 1042 and the manor was still listed in the properties owned by the Abbey of Peterborough in 1086, according to the great survey now known as the Domesday Book, when King William assessed the wealth of his newly won lands after the Norman Conquest.

THE GRAMMAR SCHOOL AND THE HIGH SCHOOL 1922 72243

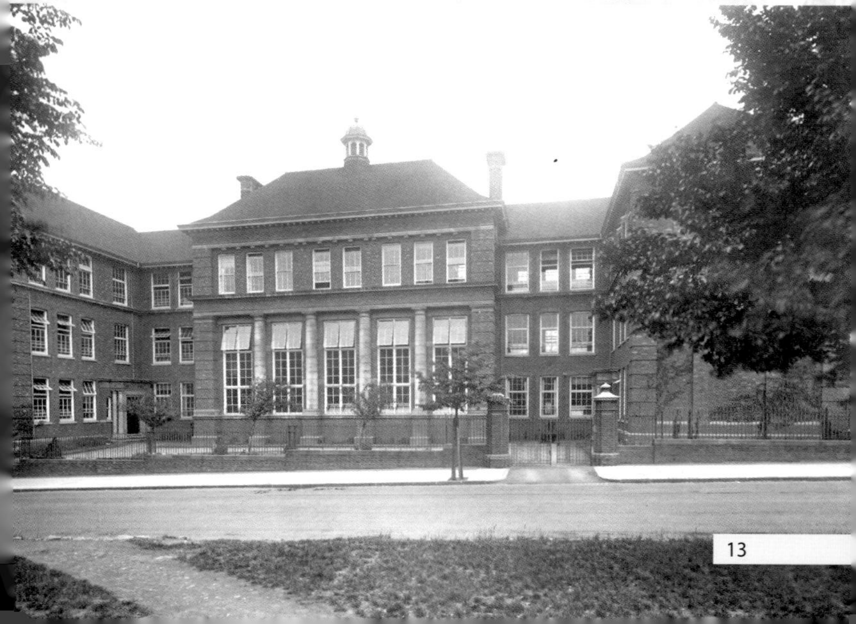

The approach to Kettering's parish church shown in photograph K13080, opposite, is from Sheep Street, along a gravelled tree-lined avenue through memorial gates. These were erected in memory of the Roughton family, who served the town as doctors continuously from 1738 until 1933; the fourth Dr Roughton set up the general hospital, which opened in 1891. The Roughton Memorial Gates are decorated with a coat of arms on the left-hand pillar and a brief history of the family's connections with Kettering on the right-hand pillar. The avenue leads to the superb west tower of the church of St Peter and St Paul, whose grandeur recalls the pre-boot and shoe era of the sheep trade, from which the town gained its earlier wealth. The Perpendicular tower is 179ft high, with a battlemented spire, and was probably built before the nave, as buttresses appear inside the building. There are four stages with the upper, bell stage, having three openings. The church underwent some restoration in the 19th century, but the basic tall and elegant structure is largely unaltered. The buildings shown to the right of the church in photograph 72239 on page 45 were part of the District Council offices, which have now been demolished.

One of Kettering's most successful businessmen in the shoe industry was Thomas Gotch, who set up as a shoe-maker and leather-dresser in 1786. His home-working enterprise grew to a big business employing many out-workers as he fulfilled army contracts during the Napoleonic Wars. He ran the business from Chesham House in Lower Street. This elegant building of 1762 is still standing, although it is now in a car park.

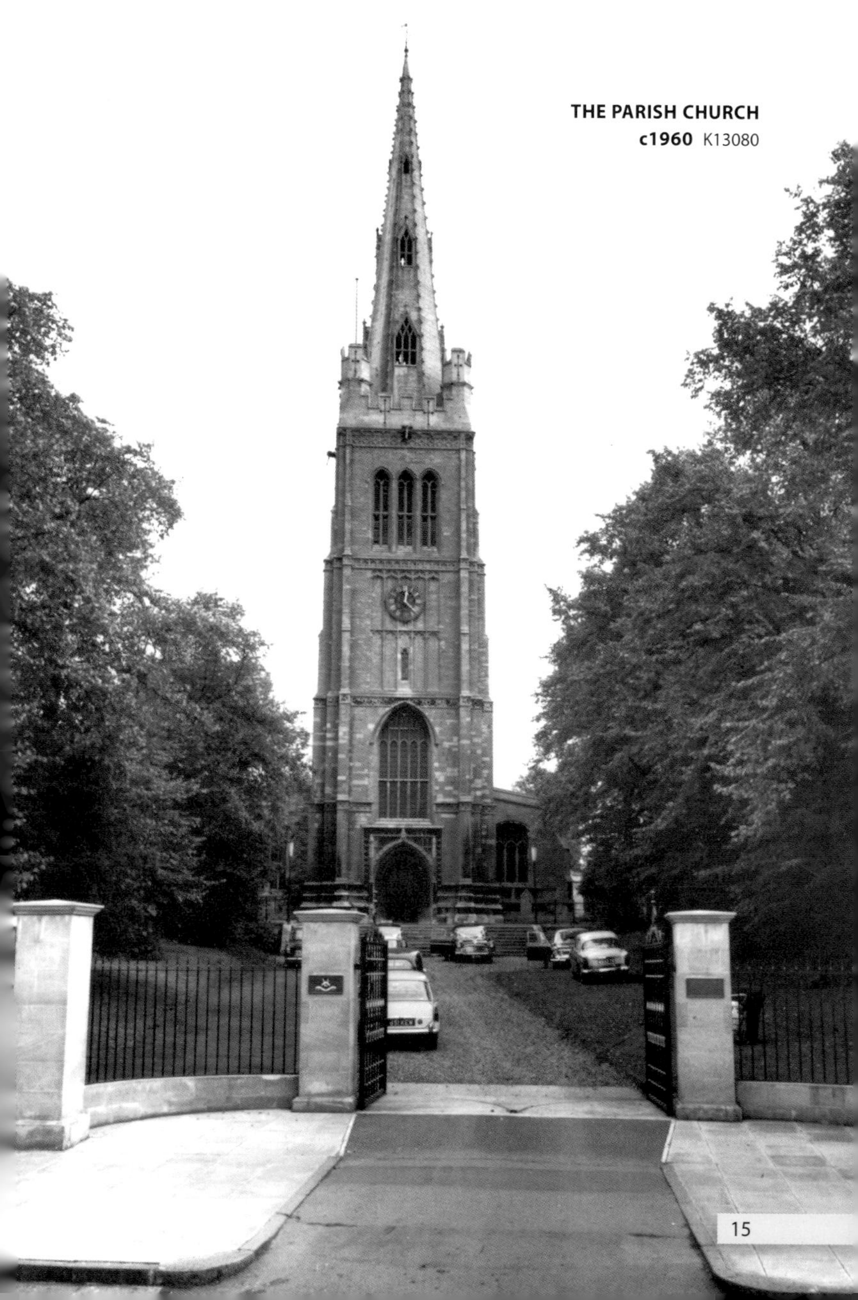

THE PARISH CHURCH
c1960 K13080

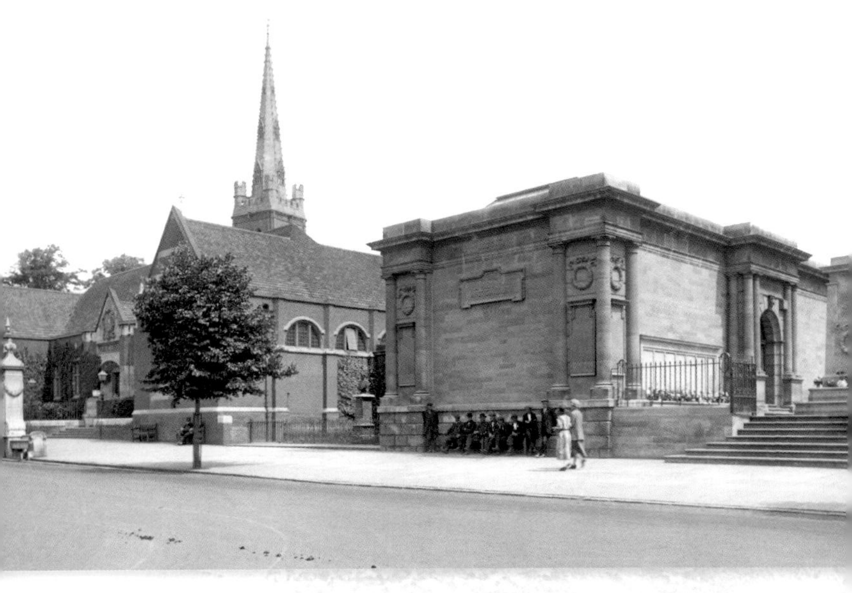

THE ALFRED EAST GALLERY 1922 72244

Kettering's art gallery at the entrance to Sheep Street opened in 1913 and was named after a noted local artist, Sir Alfred East. The building, shown in photograph 72244, above, looks like an outsize tomb, so it is appropriate that soon after the gallery opened Sir Alfred died, and lay in state there like a king while Kettering people filed past him. The gallery had been built to house a collection of paintings that he was to leave to the town; how uncanny that he should become one of the first exhibits! At the end of the 19th century Sir Alfred East was an establishment artist - he was an associate of the Royal Academy and President of the Royal Society of British Artists - yet he had wild moments too. He spent summers in Cornwall, usually in St Ives, or visiting another well-known Kettering painter, Thomas Cooper Gotch, who lived and worked in Newlyn. Their loose vigorous paintings in sunlit colours attempted to bring the brilliance of French Impressionism into England. A bronze bust of Sir Alfred rules over a tiny garden set between the Alfred East Gallery and the neighbouring library.

When the railway station was opened in 1857, it also opened the way to mass production: the boot and shoe industry took off with the trains; products could be transported quickly and cheaply to markets much further afield, and many shoe-makers who had been trained by the Gotches set up their own independent workshops, and then factories, throughout Kettering.

Photograph K13071, below, shows St Edward's Roman Catholic Church, which was completed in 1940 although the redbrick geometrical design looks post-war. Fronting London Road, it faces the entrance on St Mary's Road where the Technical College was to be built in 1955. The houses on the right of the photograph, examples of the late Victorian baronial style, are an interesting contrast. It is thought that their stone came from buildings in Gold Street which were demolished in 1887.

THE ROMAN CATHOLIC CHURCH c1965 K13071

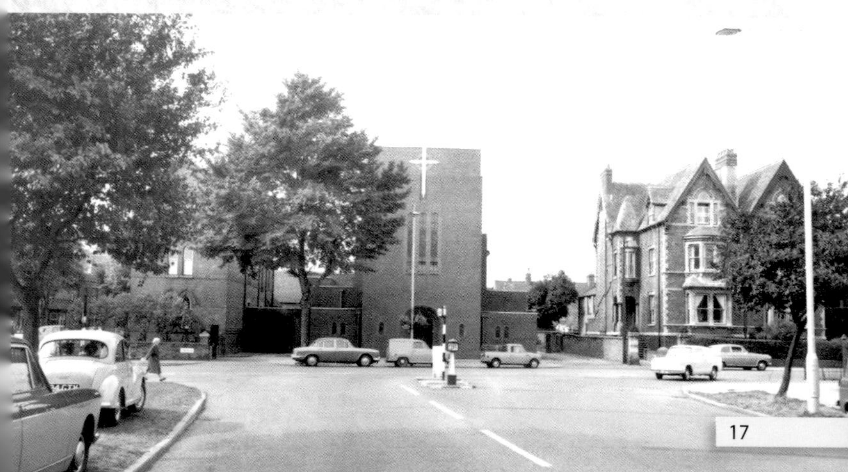

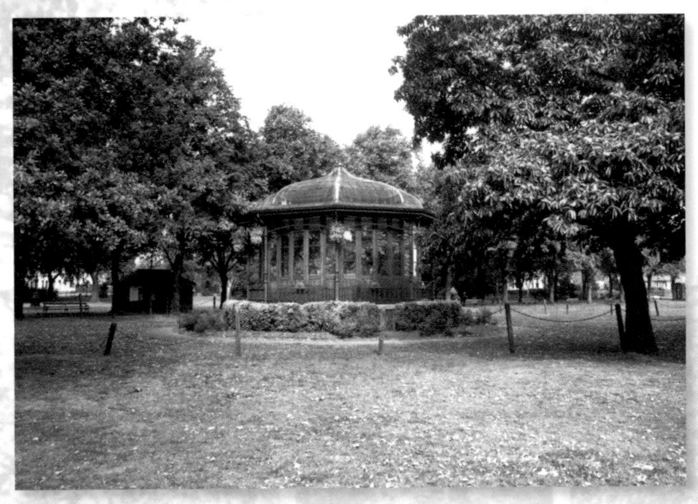

ROCKINGHAM ROAD PLEASURE PARK, THE BANDSTAND c1955 K13058

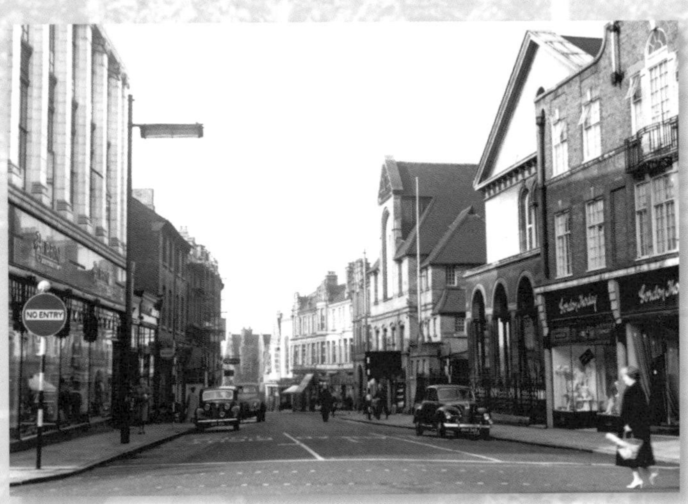

GOLD STREET c1950 K13042

Charles Wicksteed founded an engineering works in Kettering in 1876. He had started work in Leeds, where he designed steam ploughs. Beginning with the manufacture of machine tools, he went on to design a motor gearbox in 1907, but in 1914 his factory made munitions. He believed in the nationalisation of land, and when he became a town councillor he persuaded the council to buy land in the growing residential area off Rockingham Road. It provided a play area for children from the terraced streets round the factories, as well as from those avenues built by the Co-op to the north.

Boot- and shoe-making were major industries of Northamptonshire for many centuries. This was influenced by two major factors - lush grassland and extensive forests. The bark of oak trees provided the tanning materials, and the flocks and herds grazing on the Northamptonshire grassland provided the latter. The Northamptonshire boot- and shoe-making towns teemed with footwear factories and all the trades associated with them: lasts, heels, laces and machinery were also made in workshops. From 1850 until 1950 leather was Kettering's business, but when cheaper foreign imports flooded the markets, the footwear factories closed. In 1934 there were 29 shoe manufacturers and over 30 workshops in the town connected with leather, but now there is only a handful of businesses associated with shoe-making. Those factories which have not been pulled down have been turned into apartment blocks, and the sites of others have become new housing developments or supermarkets.

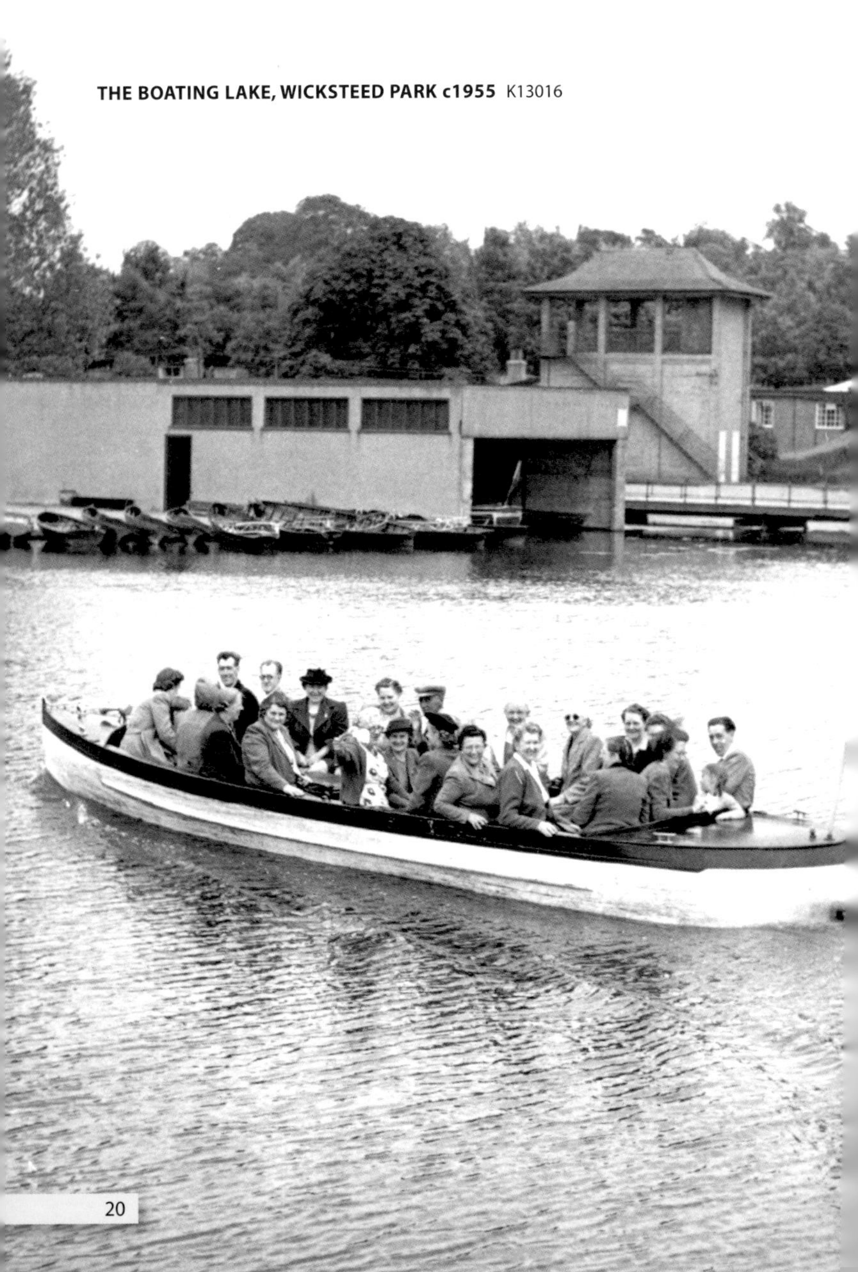

THE BOATING LAKE, WICKSTEED PARK c1955 K13016

The founder of the Timpson Shoes chain of shops was William Timpson, who was one of the rags-to-riches patriarchs of Victorian Kettering. He came from a family in the weaving trade, which was suffering in the mid 19th century from advances in machinery that put home-workers out of business. William went to work from the age of eight, making leather laces for the Gotch factory. His elder brother Charles had started a shoe shop in Manchester, and in 1860, at the age of eleven, William set off to join him. In the early railway age there was a great criss-crossing of lines and William got lost in the system, ending up with no money on a platform in Sheffield. The rest of the story is like the plot of a Dickens novel. As William stood there crying, an old gentleman asked him what had happened; after hearing the boy's story the old man took him on the correct train and delivered him to his brother, and then vanished before the Timpsons thought of asking his name. After this, the young William flourished. He realised that his Lancashire customers had wider-than-average feet, so when he had to return south through ill health he started a shoe-making workshop in Kettering to make wide fittings for the northern market. He began work in a former silk-weaving mill in Market Street and his fortune was made. William Timpson never forgot the old man who had rescued him in 1860, and at the firm's annual lunch a toast would be made 'to the unknown benefactor' until William died in 1929.

Close to the cattle market, the George Hotel was a popular farmers' 'ordinary'. Originally called the Cock, the name was probably changed in a fit of patriotic fervour in the 18th century. In 1896 it was advertised as having 'ten loose boxes, a five stall, a four stall and two stall stables, two coach houses, a cow house for eight cows, a large yard and a pig yard'. Behind the façade of the shops the car park of the hotel has supplanted the stockyard.

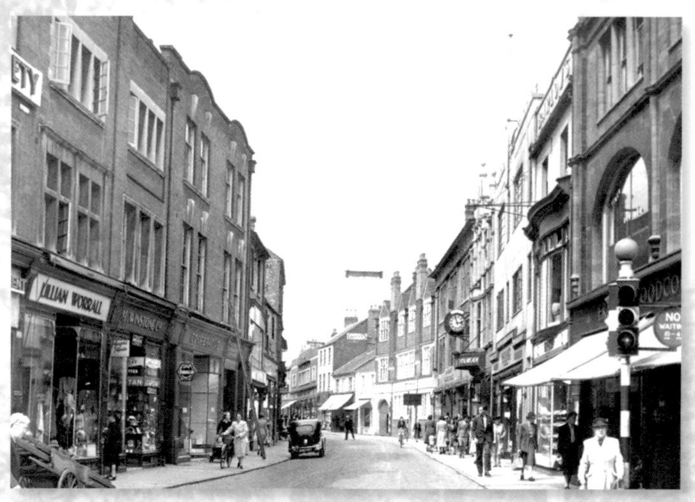

NEWLAND STREET c1955 K13019

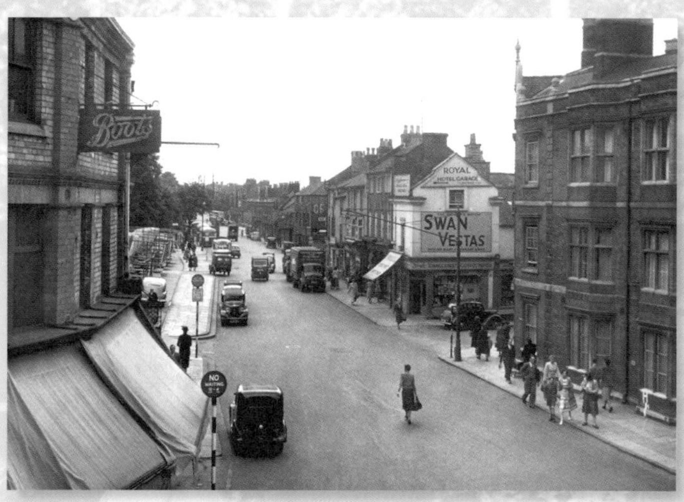

THE MARKET PLACE c1950 K13026

The Co-operative movement was very vigorous in Kettering, and Newland Street became its showpiece. The first shop in town even pre-dated the famous Rochdale Co-op pioneers of 1848: it was established in 1829, when the town was going through hard times with little employment in the weaving trade, and before the manufacture of boots and shoes had become the main industry. Kettering at that time had around 3,000 inhabitants, living in primitive cottages. The shop failed, probably because it was underfunded. In 1866 the Co-op started again with 60 members, only two of whom could afford to pay the £1 share; the others invested at 4 pence a week. The 'shop' was a front room of a house in the High Street, and a committee member walked to Northampton and back to buy the first orders. The Co-op survived, and the members opened their first real shop in 1868. They expanded to two shops, and set up their own bakery. Kettering Co-operative gathered momentum and soon had an educational section, its own magazine, a choral society and flower shows; there were even scholarships to help keep bright children at school. Kettering Co-op (KICS) ended with seventeen shops all over the town and in nearby villages. Increasingly self-sufficient, the Co-op even became landlords at the end of the 19th century, when they built 100 houses on the northern reaches of Kettering. As supermarkets and multiple stores opened in Kettering the Co-op became less important, although outlying stores in large villages remained. A KICS supermarket was finally opened in the 'new' area of Northfield Avenue, which replaced all the various stores of the past. By 1978 KICS had to amalgamate with Leicestershire Co-op.

The building with the Swan Vestas advertisement shown in photograph K13026, opposite, housed Poole's, tobacconist and newsagent, in the 1950s, but this was once the premises of the ill-fated Gotch Bank. This was run by John Cooper Gotch, son of the successful shoe-maker and leather dresser Thomas Gotch, but the bank had to close abruptly in 1857 through mismanagement.

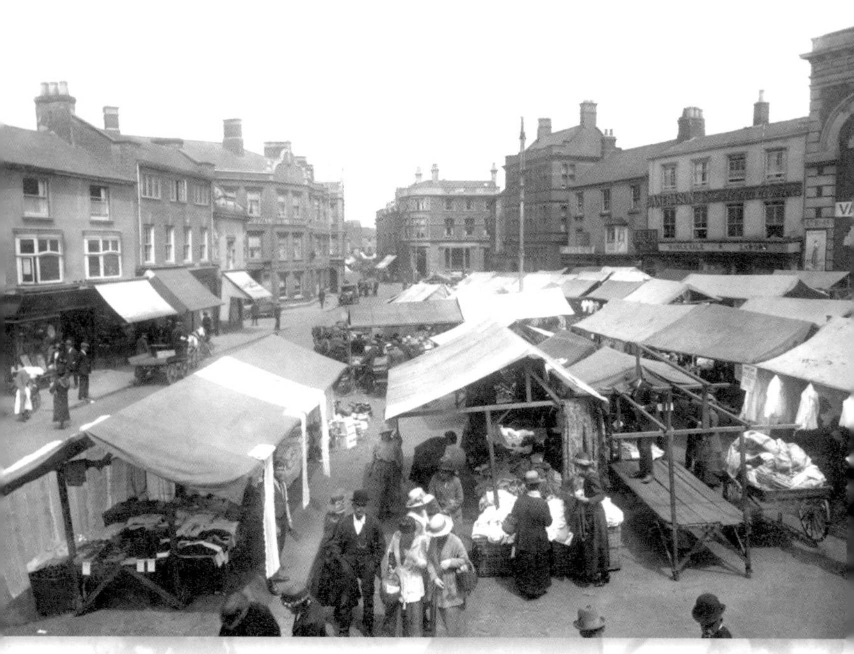

THE MARKET 1922 72233

Kettering's Corn Exchange became the Palace cinema and theatre in the early 1900s after a short spell as a lending library. The Palace was owned by John Covington, who tried to combine both functions in the days of silent films by placing an actor and actress behind a curtain to read accompanying dialogue. In 1922 the building was sold and re-named but remained a cinema (seen on the right of photograph 72233, above), presenting a continuous performance from 6.15pm to 10.30pm. On Saturday afternoons there was a children's matinee, when there were uproarious fights between the circle and the stalls. The building later became a billiards hall, and is now used as shops.

The Old Post Office Buildings can be seen on the right of Gold Street in photograph 72231, below. Designed by Gotch & Saunders, they were faced with distinctive red terracotta and were built in 1887. The General Post Office was an important feature of the block, which had an arcade forming a passage through to Richard Leys and Tanners Lane behind. All was to be changed in 1974, when the Newborough Centre was erected. There was enormous opposition to the demolition plans. The Kettering Civic Society suggested that the new shopping complex could be built behind the Victorian parade, but this plan was ignored and it was pulled down; in its place now there is an indoor mall, fronted by Boots the Chemist.

GOLD STREET 1922 72231

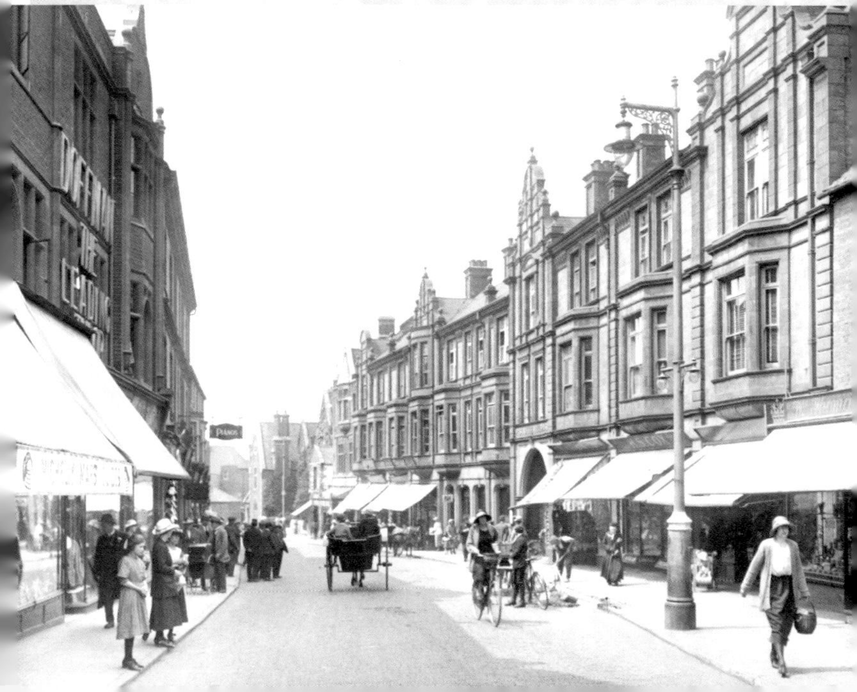

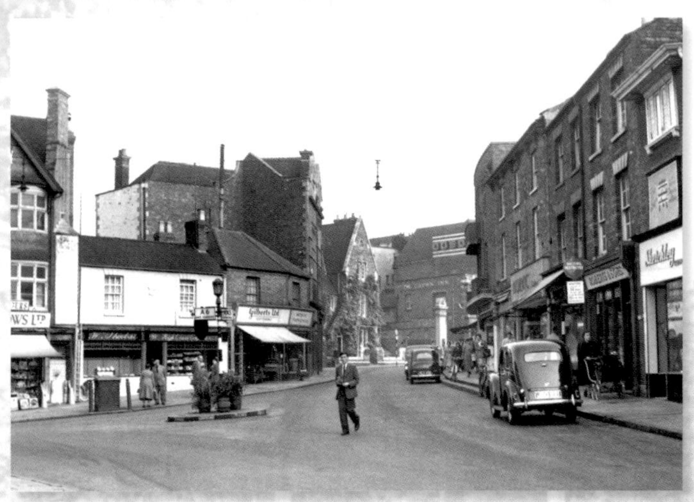

BACKHOUSE HILL c1955 K13044

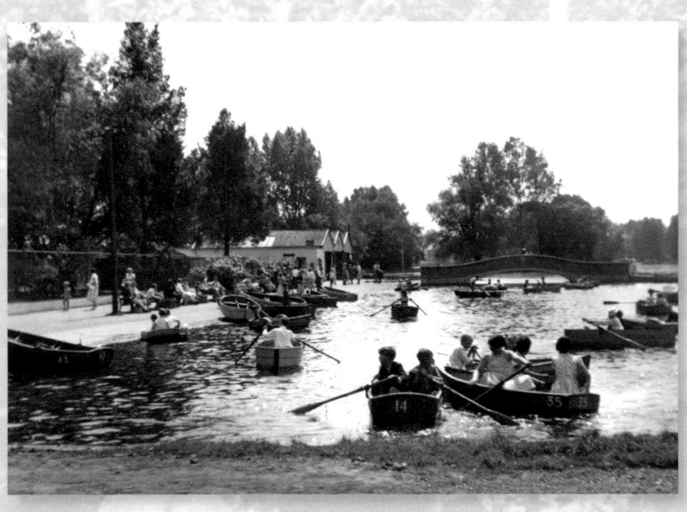

THE BOATING LAKE, WICKSTEED PARK c1965 K13507

The friendly triangle seen in photograph K13044, opposite, where the High Street and Gold Street meet, no longer exists. The area was redeveloped in the 1960s, and now there is a slightly changed layout, with a pedestrianised 'island' with seats and shrubs replacing the old road junction. The original communal town bakehouse stood here in the 16th century. Bell & Billows, on the left-hand side of the photograph, was an ironmongers, built in 1889 and demolished in 1968. The window displays there always attracted enormous male attention, with large rows of sheath knives and air-rifles. Next door was the baker's shop of W Theobald, which later moved into Low Street.

After the First World War, the Kettering manufacturer Charles Wicksteed diverted from munitions into playground equipment. It was a time when enlightened councils were setting up public parks and recreation grounds with swings and slides. He shared his success with Kettering by buying 150 acres on the edge of town on the way to the village of Barton Seagrave. By 1921 he had turned it into an enormous playground for children, Wicksteed Park; it had two boating lakes, and a model railway. The smaller lake, for younger children, was separated from the larger one by a hump-backed bridge. Coaches brought visitors to the park from all over the East Midlands.

John Cooper Gotch, the son of Thomas Gotch, was probably the most influential man in the town in the mid 19th century, not only as a shoe manufacturer and proprietor of Gotch Bank but also as a leading Liberal and Nonconformist. In 1844 he arranged a visit to the town by Queen Victoria, who stayed briefly in Room 12 at the White Hart, which was later re-named the Royal Hotel in her honour.

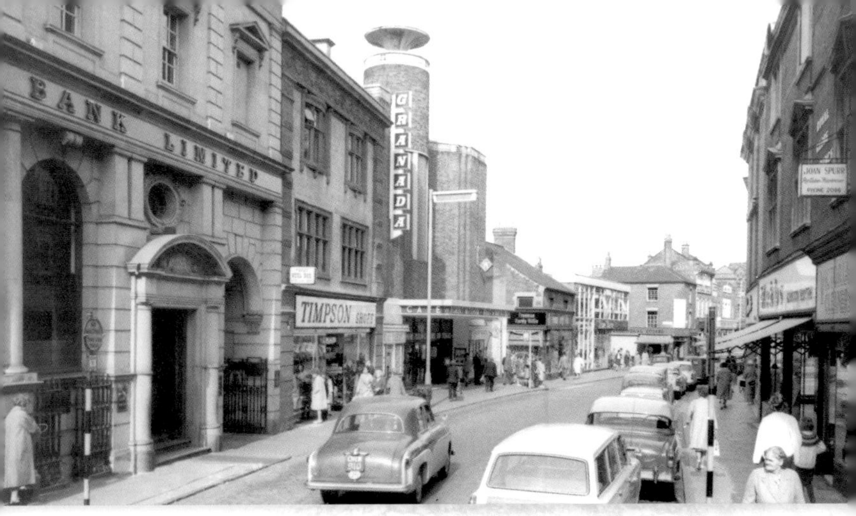

HIGH STREET c1960 K13065

Photograph K13065, above, shows the High Street c1960. Timpson Shoes can be seen on the left-hand side, next to the Granada cinema; Timpson Shoes had branches all over Britain, but the shoes were made in Kettering. The factory was just round the corner in Market Street until trade increased so much that it was not big enough to cope with the demand, and in 1921 one of the most modern factories in Britain, an enormous glass structure like a Crystal Palace, was built beside green playing fields in North Park, which was then near the edge of Kettering. Timpsons had become gigantic by the 1950s, supplying 22,000 pairs of shoes a week for 262 retail shops, but gradually demand for British-made footwear decreased, and Timpsons sold their great glass factory in 1972.

The Manor House was still called the Abbot's House in the early 18th century; it may have been preceded by the monastic buildings from which Kettering grew. Largely Georgian, it now houses the town museum, where one of the more unusual exhibits is a mummified cat.

A few miles from Kettering, at Rushton, is one of England's most unusual buildings, the Triangular Lodge, seen in photograph R272010, below. Almost a folly, this was actually built for serious reasons by Sir Thomas Tresham in 1593. It was officially erected as a rabbit warrener's lodge, but in reality it was a secret reflection of Tresham's Roman Catholic faith in a zealously Protestant era, after his release from a long imprisonment for being a 'Papist'. This stone manifestation of Tresham's Catholicism takes its name from the fact that everything about it is triangular; it is constructed according to a factor of three, symbolising the Holy Trinity, with three sides, three floors, three windows on each floor, and three gables. Sir Thomas Tresham's son, Francis, was later to be implicated in the Gunpowder Plot.

RUSHTON, THE TRIANGULAR LODGE c1955 R272010

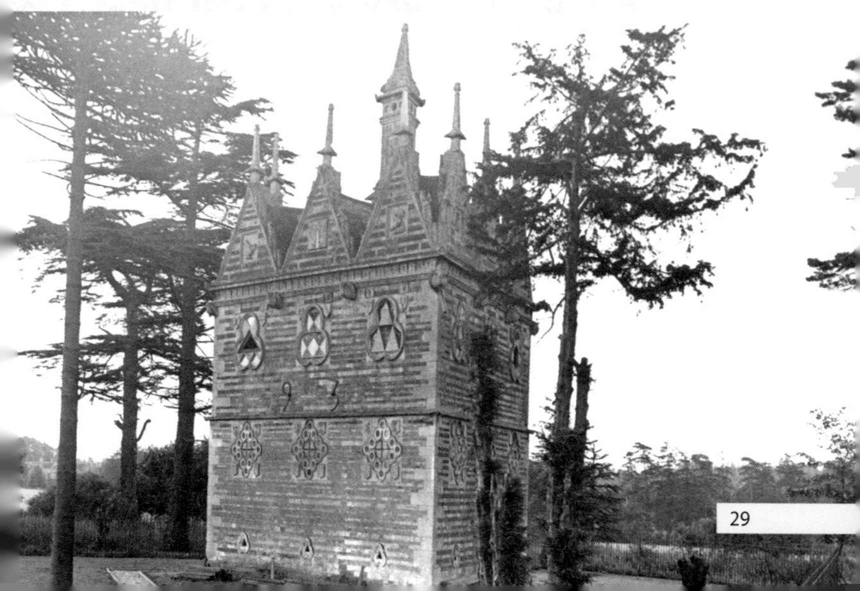

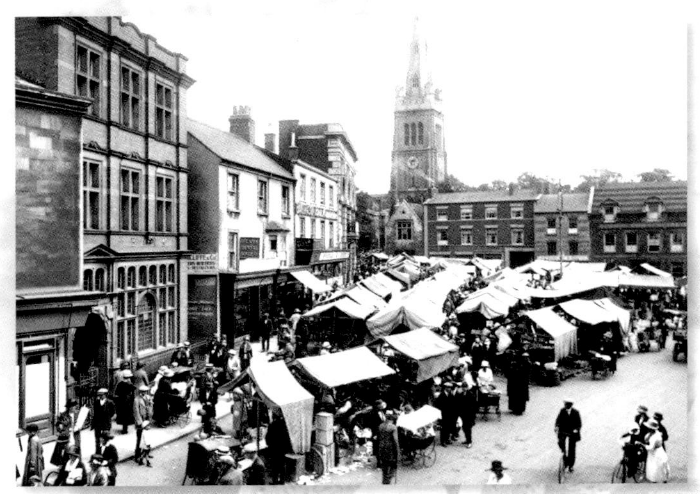

THE MARKET 1922 72232

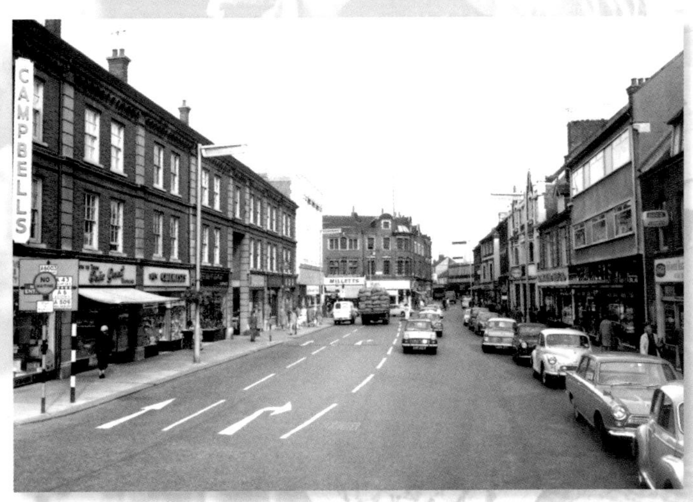

SILVER STREET c1960 K13064

Photograph 72232, opposite, shows Kettering market in 1922. The south side of the market, facing the camera, was bordered by a row of buildings which were demolished in the 1930s. The gabled stone building in front of the church housed the Market Offices, and was also a drop-in centre for the unemployed; it was built of stone from the Session House, which had stood in the market until 1805. Paynes the bakers were in the pale upright building with advertisements for wedding cakes on the frontage. They were the first commercial ice-cream makers in Kettering. The Albion Temperance Hotel is nearest the road. When this block was demolished it was replaced by a car park.

At one time quarrying was an important local industry, and iron ore was produced from open cast mines in nearby villages and on the outskirts of the town itself. 3ft-gauge railways threaded the area, carrying ore to blast furnaces situated between the railway and Rockingham Road. The furnaces were worked between 1878 and 1954, and although Kettering people became accustomed to the red glow in the sky all night and day, it became a special landmark for rail passengers travelling past at night. The quarry sites were filled in after their usefulness was over, and some became farmland whilst others were used for housing developments.

Kettering's parish church has a peal of twelve bells, which is one of the largest in the country; nearby residents are no doubt grateful that shutters to the belfry openings can be closed to reduce noise levels during bell-ringing practice! Three of the original bells were cast by Thomas Eayre (1691-1757), a member of the well-known Eayre family of Kettering bellfounders which is commemorated in the name of Belfry Lane, off Wadcroft, which was formerly Bellfounders Lane.

Kettering's economic base of small workshops and independent tradesmen fostered a strong tradition of radicalism and religious nonconformity. This anti-establishment attitude was manifested as early as 1666, when a 'Great Meeting' was formed by John Maidwell, who was then the rector of the parish church. Maidment chose to leave the established Church to form his own Nonconformist chapel in Hazelwood Lane. 20 years later there was another breakaway from the established Church when the 'Little Meeting' set up a Baptist chapel in Gold Street.

Like many Kettering buildings, the Alfred East Gallery was designed by Gotch & Saunders. Gotch & Saunders were responsible for much of town's architecture, which is often brick-built with stone facings round the windows and doors, in a solid, unassuming and timeless style. Because one firm was pre-eminent in Kettering from the 1890s until the 1930s, the town developed in a pleasantly uniform way. John Alfred Gotch was an expert on Elizabethan and Jacobean buildings, and he was also interested in old building materials and techniques. He was the brother of Thomas Cooper Gotch, the painter with whom Alfred East stayed in Cornwall; his other two brothers stayed in the boot and shoe business and they were closely involved with the growth of education in the town - a comprehensive school is named after Henry Gotch.

Many of Kettering's old street names have disappeared, or been changed over the centuries: Market Street was once called Parkstile Lane, and Walker Lane was once known as Pudding Bag Lane because of its cul-de-sac shape. Gold Street was known as Paul Street in the 18th century, named after two surgeons, Hugh and Matthew Paul, who were father and son. Meadow Road has had several names, Mill Lane, Gas Street and, before the 19th century, Goose Pasture Lane, because geese were fattened there before being sold at market.

The parish church in Kettering has one of the tallest church spires in Northamptonshire. When Nikolaus Pevsner recorded it, he thought it had 'a curious, ungenuine look, as if it were an imitation, or re-erected'. Most of the windows in the church are clear glass, which gives the interior a light, airy atmosphere, but in the south chancel aisle there is a window formed from broken pieces of stained glass which were dug up in the grounds, and a large window showing scenes from the life of Our Lady was installed when the Lady Chapel was restored in 1927. There are also three medieval wall paintings in the church. The one of St Roch is indeciperable, but high on the walls of the clerestory, above the nave, there are some very faded relics of coloured angels.

HIGH STREET 1922 72227

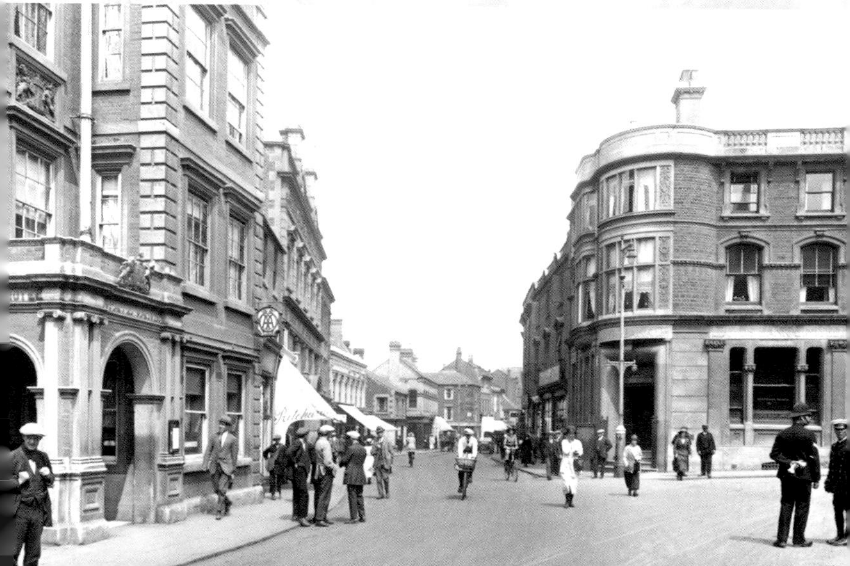

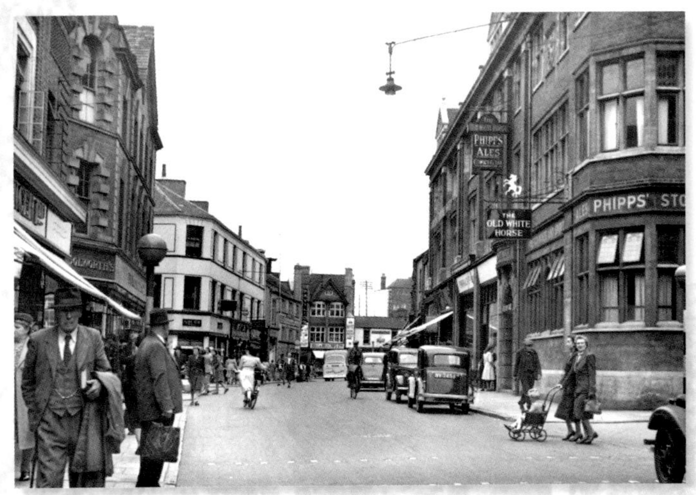

HIGH STREET c1950 K13024

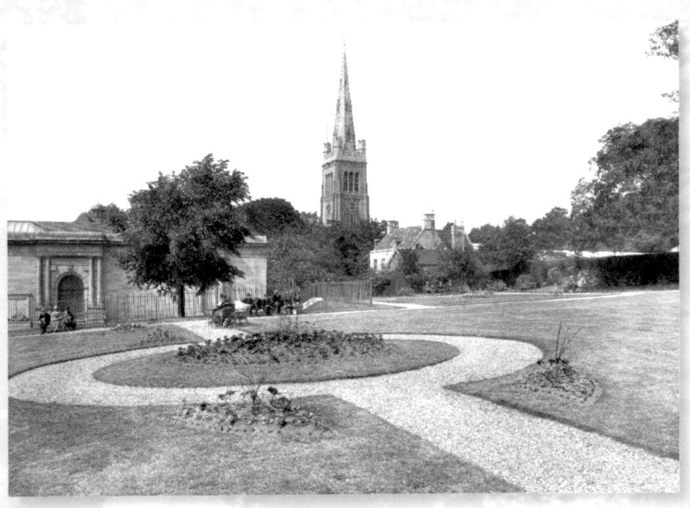

MANOR HOUSE GARDENS 1922 72246

In the middle of photograph K13044 on page 26 is the old Grammar School, with its distinctive gabled façade covered with creepers, including a luxuriant wisteria. Most schools are proud to trace their foundation back to the time of Elizabeth I, but Kettering Grammar School was too old for its origins to be recorded, although the queen did give aid to the ancient school by endowing it with some property. The original school was probably a relic of the days when there was a chantry school attached to the church. The school had a chequered history until the 19th century, with some eccentric or lazy masters, until finally there were only two or three boys left. The school was re-organised in 1854; a dynamic new master increased its popularity, and fees were charged according to the parents' means. Two years later there were so many pupils that the 'new' school seen in this photograph was built. It was finished in 1859, in the style of a Jacobean country house, with a master's lodging on one side. In spite of the new attractive premises, this school was not a success. The lively master left and was succeeded by an incompetent one, a Mr Widdowson, who did nothing to attract new pupils. Finally Mr Widdowson accepted a handsome pension and left, but now it was obvious that the school premises were no longer suitable. A new neo-Georgian building was erected in Bowling Green Road in 1913, which was large enough to house both the Grammar School for boys and a High School for girls (see photograph 72243 on page 13). The old school building became a doctor's surgery, and then council offices. It was demolished in 1964, despite considerable local opposition, to make way for a new shopping parade. In the early 1960s the Grammar School moved - again - to Windmill Avenue (where it eventually closed, and the building became the Art Department of the Tresham Institute), and the Borough Council took over the vacated 1913 building.

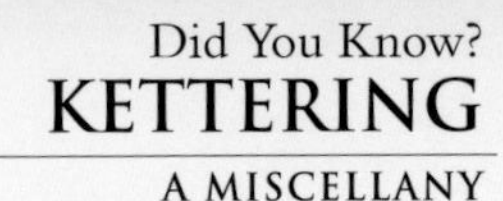

On the pavement edge near the Alfred East Gallery and the library in Sheep Street is the Dryland Memorial. Kettering owed much to its doctors, and Dr Dryland was instrumental in forming the Local Government Board in 1872. This was a precursor to the Urban Council, which in turn became the Borough Council. Dr Dryland worked hard for a more hygienic town, and especially for a pure water supply, so it is fitting that he is remembered by a drinking fountain - even if it is now empty. Not only humans were catered for by this memorial - it also incorporates a drinking trough for horses, and another trough lower down for dogs.

A public library was first opened in Kettering in 1896 in the Corn Exchange in the Market Place. It then moved to Silver Street, and finally came to rest in Sheep Street in 1904. The low brick building, with Ketton stone facings, cost £8,000. The money was given by the philanthropist Andrew Carnegie (1835-1919) who donated part of the fortune that he made in America to building libraries throughout the United Kingdom in gratitude for what he had learned in public libraries in his youth in Scotland. Kettering's library was unusual in that it was actually opened in person by Mr Carnegie, who usually preferred to stay out of the public gaze.

The Census returns for the last 200 years make interesting reading. In 1801 the population of Kettering was 12,734; by 1901 this had risen to 41,770, and by 2001 the total population was 81,842. In 1851, 137 babies in every 1,000 live births died in their first year; by 1911 the number had only slightly reduced, to 107 in every 1,000, but by 2001 the rate was only 4 every 1,000.

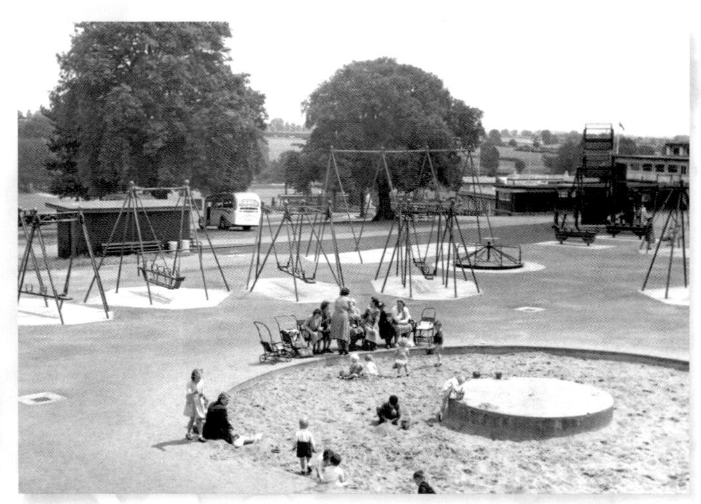

THE CHILDREN'S PLAYGROUND, WICKSTEED PARK c1955 K13008

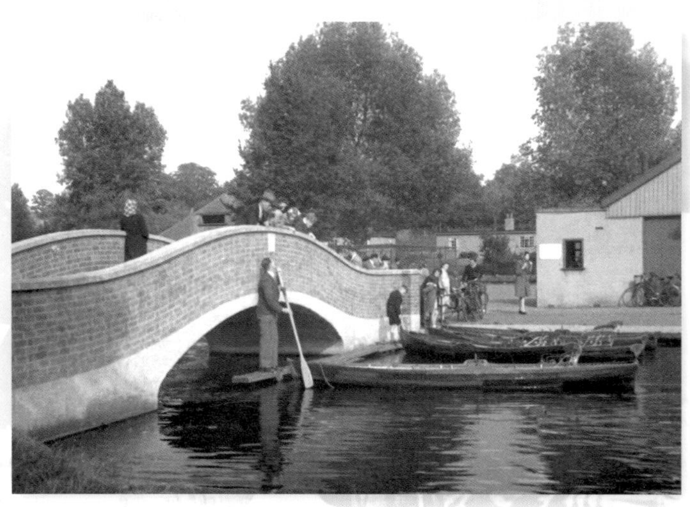

THE BRIDGE, WICKSTEED PARK c1955 K13003

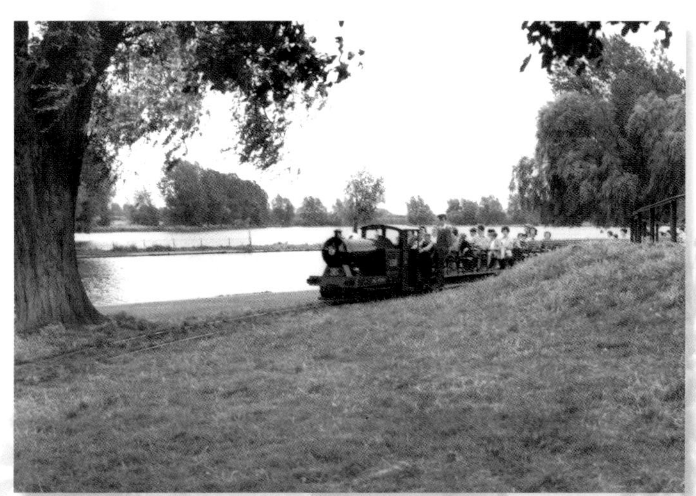

THE MINIATURE RAILWAY, WICKSTEED PARK c1960 K13051

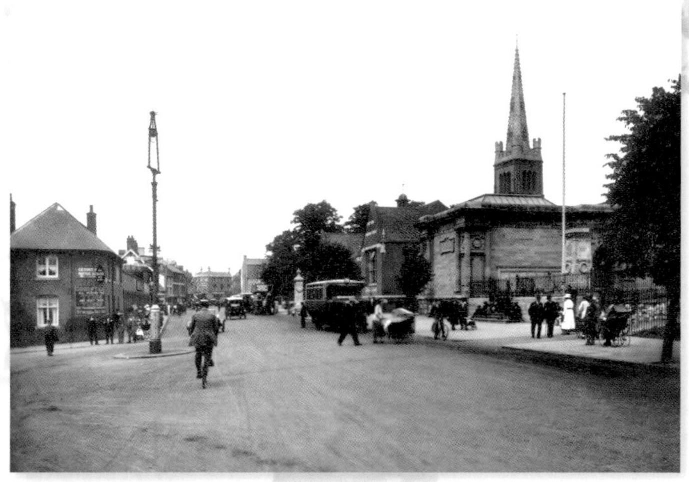

SHEEP STREET 1922 72237

Kettering's former Corn Exchange in the market place is a handsome building of 1854. When it was built, by public subscription, the Town Hall was upstairs behind the arched windows, with a lofty view of what was then the busiest part of the town. The balcony was used by speakers to address outdoor meetings, and it was from his window in the nearby White Hart (later the Royal Hotel) that the young journalist Charles Dickens watched a meeting of radical weavers in the 1830s. He was angered by seeing the local farmers and landowners riding their horses into the crowd, lashing at the protestors' faces with their boots and iron stirrups.

In the late 19th century the politically powerful Duke of Buccleuch, who lived at nearby Boughton House, bought the Royal Hotel to turn it into the local Conservative Party headquarters, and it was virtually rebuilt in the style of Kirby Hall, a great Elizabethan house in the area. In 1896 the duke sold the premises to Pickering Phipps, a Northampton brewer, and a magnificent billiards room with a stained-glass roof and ceramic name plates for the bars were added. At this time, a bill records that dinner for three people cost 7s 6d (35p). The billiards room has survived, but the public bar with engraved glass windows was pulled down in 1983, in spite of protests by the Civic Society.

Kettering once had its own small-scale car-making industry: the Robinson car was made for Robinson's garage, which opened in Montagu Street in 1905. Only three of these cars were constructed, one of which can be seen in the Manor House Museum; this car was first registered on 1 April 1910, but it was built in 1907 in an engineering works in nearby Victoria Street, which belonged to the grandfather of the garage owner, Charles Robinson. It was 12-horsepower (1884cc), and had a unique cooling system in which the exhaust gases were used to propel fresh air round the engine.

The Granada cinema, seen in the High Street in photograph K13065 on page 28, was originally the Regal, which opened in 1938, and was bought by the Granada chain in the 1950s. This exciting Art Deco building represented luxury to audiences. The auditorium was popularly supposed to seat 1,500, and there was a tearoom on the first floor. The Granada certainly knew how to entertain the public: in the early 1960s they would have a midweek change of programme, and visiting bands and pop stars gave stage shows on Sundays. The building is now a bingo hall.

Photograph 72230 on page 12 shows Hitchman's chemist shop on the left-hand side, on the corner of Silver Street and Gold Street. Their own medicines were made up in the dispensary, where they also made a well-known sulphur pill for skin problems and an 'extract of honey' hand cream. This sort of chemist often had scales for weighing babies, as well as alluring bottles of coloured liquids as window decorations. The young mothers in the photograph may well have just been getting free advice on childcare from Hitchman's. It is noticeable from the early 20th-century photographs in this book that, however poor they were, at this time both men and women wore hats when they went out, even on local errands. This corner would be dominated in the 1930s by the white Art Deco emporium of Burton's, seen on the extreme left of photograph K13042 on page 18 and to the left of Milletts in photograph K13064 on page 30.

Photograph K13058 on page 26 shows the bandstand in Rockingham Road Pleasure Park which was built in the 1930s. A regular programme of music was played here, and sometimes there were concerts by the famous brass band of Munn & Felton. This band had been started by Frederick Felton, a partner in a boot factory. He was another of Kettering's self-made men, who started his career selling bootlaces door-to-door. He had also been a bandsman in the Salvation Army, so he was experienced when he set up his works' band, which went on to win prizes throughout the world.

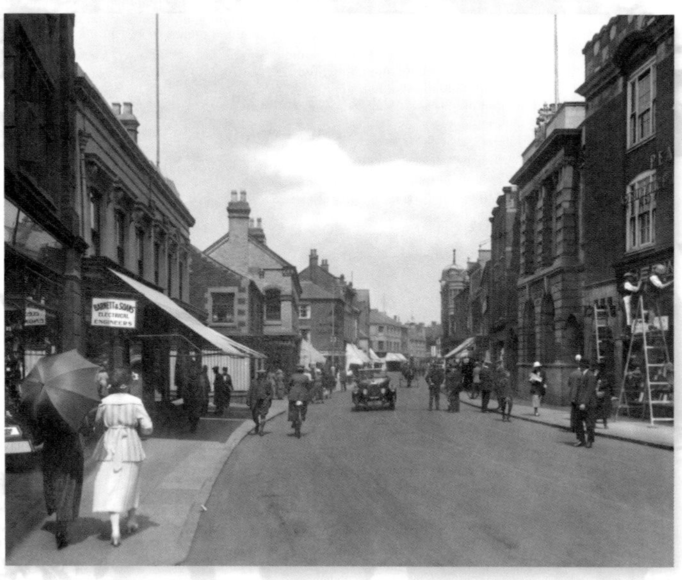

HIGH STREET 1922 72229

An organisation as influential as Kettering Co-operative had to have important premises, and a magnificent drapery store was opened in Newland Street in 1893, with oriel windows echoing those of the Rising Sun in nearby Silver Street. An arcade and central store were opened in the 1920s, linking Newland and Montagu Streets (we can see the Central Arcade entrance porch in photograph K13019 on page 22). The building included a large meeting hall and on the day of the opening ceremony, held at a time when the first Labour government was in office, the Prime Minister (Ramsay MacDonald) sent a jocular message to KICS, asking them not to deprive him of his whole cabinet, for three government ministers were attending the event!

As he grew older, Charles Wicksteed would often visit Wicksteed Park in a two-seater car, with his terrier, Jerry, sitting on the passenger seat. In 1927 Jerry disappeared on one of these outings. He was never found, and in his memory his master had a statue erected in the gardens of the park, with a commemorative verse:

'Closely bound to a human heart,
Little brown dog, you had your part
In the levelling, building, staying of streams
In the Park that arose from your Master's dreams.'

SPORTING KETTERING

Ralph Bainbridge is one of the leading figures in the history of Kettering Rugby Club. Among his achievements were five years as club captain, during which time the team had a run of 52 games unbeaten.

Kettering Town FC has a long and distinguished history, and is one of the oldest and best-known clubs never to have played in the Football League. The club was founded in 1872, and has been professional for over 100 years. Kettering FC has had a number of well-known managers, and two in particular are major figures in the English game:
Ron Atkinson, who later went on to manage Manchester United, was manager of Kettering from 1971-74. He was very successful, leading the Poppies to two consecutive promotions, before being recruited by League club Cambridge United. From Cambridge he went on to manage a string of big League clubs.
Derek Dougan, who made his name as a top striker for Wolverhampton Wanderers, was another household name to be manager at Rockingham Road. His spell in charge was most notable for an audacious attempt to introduce shirt advertising to the English game. In January 1976 Kettering took to the field in shirts showing the name of Kettering Tyres. This led to an FA fine, and Town were eventually forced to remove the advertising. Dougan, though, had seen how things would change, and within a few years the FA allowed shirt advertising. Sadly, when the ban was lifted Kettering were unable to find a sponsor.

Famous players produced by Kettering Town FC:

Eddie Habgood
He was sold to Arsenal for £950 in 1927. He won five championship medals in the great Arsenal teams of the 1930s, and was club captain. He also captained England in 21 of his 30 matches.

Scott Endersby
He became the youngest ever player to play in an FA Cup match when he turned out for the Poppies against Tilbury on 26 November 1977, aged 15.

Andy Hunt, the striker for Charlton Athletic Football Club, started his career at Kettering Town FC.

QUIZ QUESTIONS

Answers on page 48.

1. Some stained-glass windows in Kettering's parish church depict which saints, and why are these particularly appropriate to the town?

2. Why is there a statue of St Christopher in the parish church?

3. A car that can now be seen in the Manor House Museum was commissioned from a local car-maker, Charles Robinson, in 1907 with an interesting specification - what was unusual about it?

4. What was made at the Kaycee factory, and how did it get this name?

5. What is the connection between Kettering and the popular television series 'The Darling Buds of May', which starred David Jason and a young Catherine Zeta Jones?

6. Before the modern age of 24-hour convenience stores and flexible licensing laws, where in Kettering at one time could you legally buy a pint of beer in the early hours of the morning?

7. With which city is Kettering twinned?

8. How did the area of Wadcroft, off the High Street, get its name?

9. How did Montagu Street get its name?

10. What is the link between Kettering, King Arthur and the Lady of the Lake?

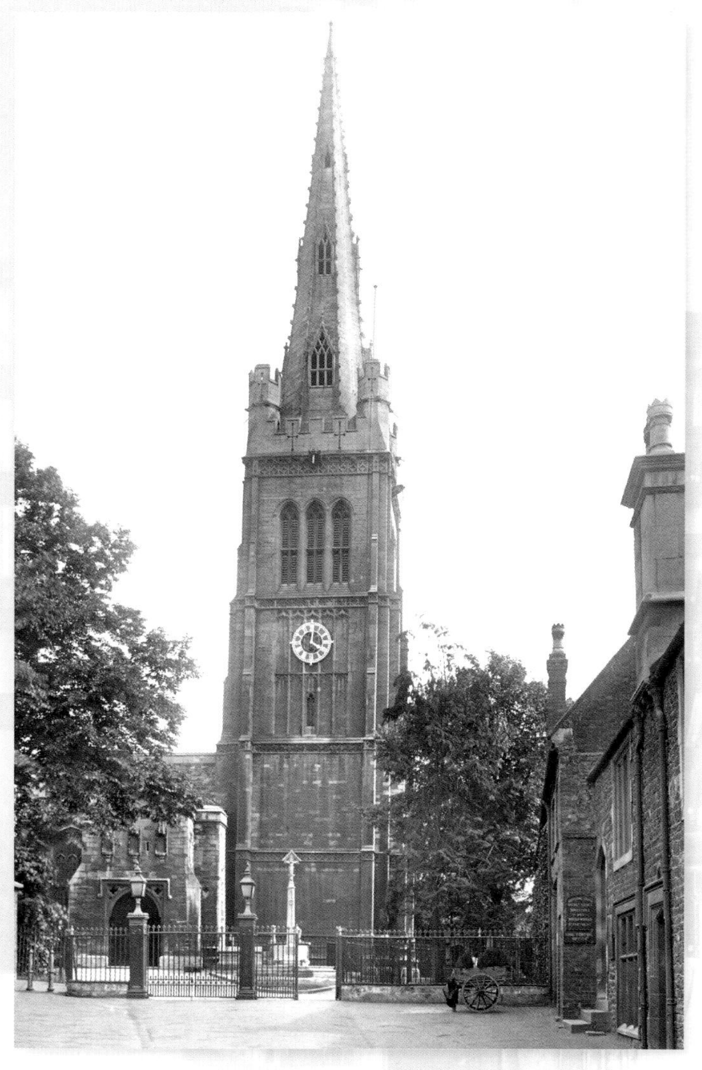

THE PARISH CHURCH AND MEMORIAL CROSS 1922 72239

RECIPE

NORTHAMPTONSHIRE PUDDING

Ingredients

110g/4oz plain flour
75g/3oz caster sugar
50g/2oz butter or margarine
2 eggs
2 tablespoonfuls raspberry jam

Sieve the flour. Cream the butter or margarine and sugar together until light and fluffy, and gradually beat in the eggs, adding a tablespoonful of flour to prevent the mixture curdling. Fold in the remaining flour, and stir in one tablespoonful of the jam. Place the remaining jam in the bottom of a greased pudding basin, and pour the pudding mixture into the basin. Cover with pleated greaseproof paper and foil. Place the pudding basin in a large saucepan of boiling water and steam for about 2 hours, topping up the water with more boiling water when necessary. When cooked, turn out on to a serving dish, and serve hot with custard or cream.

RECIPE

NORTHAMPTONSHIRE CHEESECAKES

Small cheesecakes were traditionally made in Northamptonshire to be eaten at sheep-shearing time.

Ingredients

225g/8oz shortcrust pastry
175g/6oz curd cheese or cream cheese
50g/2oz butter or margarine
2 eggs
75g/3oz caster sugar
115g/4oz currants
Finely grated rind of 1 lemon
¼ teaspoonful almond essence
½ teaspoonful ground nutmeg

Preheat the oven to 180 degrees C/350 degrees F/Gas Mark 4.

Roll out the pastry on a lightly floured surface, and use it to line 14-16 lightly greased patty tins. In a bowl, beat the curd or cream cheese until it is smooth. Put the butter or margarine into a saucepan with the sugar and eggs and heat gently, stirring all the time, until the mixture has thickened - be careful not to allow it to boil. Remove the pan from the heat, and stir in the curd or cream cheese, the currants, lemon rind and almond essence, making sure that the ingredients are well combined. Fill the patty tins with the mixture, dust the cheesecakes with a little ground nutmeg and bake for 20-25 minutes until well risen. Serve hot or cold.

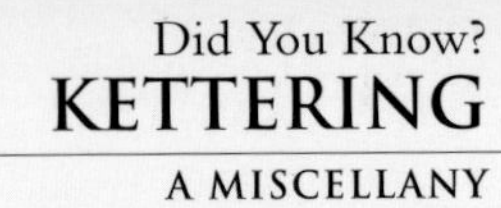

QUIZ ANSWERS

1. Most of the windows in the church are clear glass, but a few stained-glass windows made in 1963 include depictions of Saint Crispin and Saint Crispianus, who were the patron saints of shoemakers; these are reminders of Kettering's history of boot- and shoe-making.

2. During the Second World War, the United States Airforce had a base at nearby Grafton Underwood. On their return from forays over Germany, the pilots used the high spire of Kettering's parish church as a landmark on their way home. The statue of St Christopher, patron saint of travellers, in the church was their gift, and remains as a moving memorial to them.

3. The Robinson car in the Manor House Museum was commissioned in 1907 by the fourth Dr Roughton to practice in the town. The two-seater had an extra-large tool box built across the back which held the doctor's medical kit. The box was designed so that it could also be used as an emergency operating table if necessary.

4. The name derives from 'Kettering Co-operative', and for many years the Kaycee factory (run by the Co-operative in Field Street) made clothing. Co-op suits were made to measure for £2 7s 6d. One of the Co-op shops in the town, in Newland Street, can be seen in photograph K13019 on page 22. The Kaycee factory closed in 1975.

5. The television series 'The Darling Buds of May' was based on a number of books about the Larkin family which were written by H E Bates. This prolific and popular author was once a pupil at Kettering Grammar School.

6. The Fleur-de-Lys public house in Newland Street, popularly called the Flue, once had a licence to serve early morning alcohol to furnace workers coming off the night shift.

7. Kettering is twinned with the city of Kettering in Ohio in the USA, which was named after one of its citizens, Charles F Kettering, the inventor of the automobile self-starter.

8. In Saxon times the area now known as Wadcroft was probably the croft (enclosed land or smallholding) where wad (woad) was grown. The woad plant was used to make a blue dye for colouring cloth.

9. The name of Montagu Street commemorates the surname of the Dukes of Buccleuch, originally Scottish landowners whose family name was Scott-Montagu. The Buccleuchs' Northamptonshire estate is close to Kettering, and parts of the town are named after family titles: Dalkeith Place and Buccleuch Street.

10. Two locomotives on the miniature railway in Wicksteed Park in its early days were called 'King Arthur' and 'The Lady of the Lake.'

HIGH STREET c1950 K13023

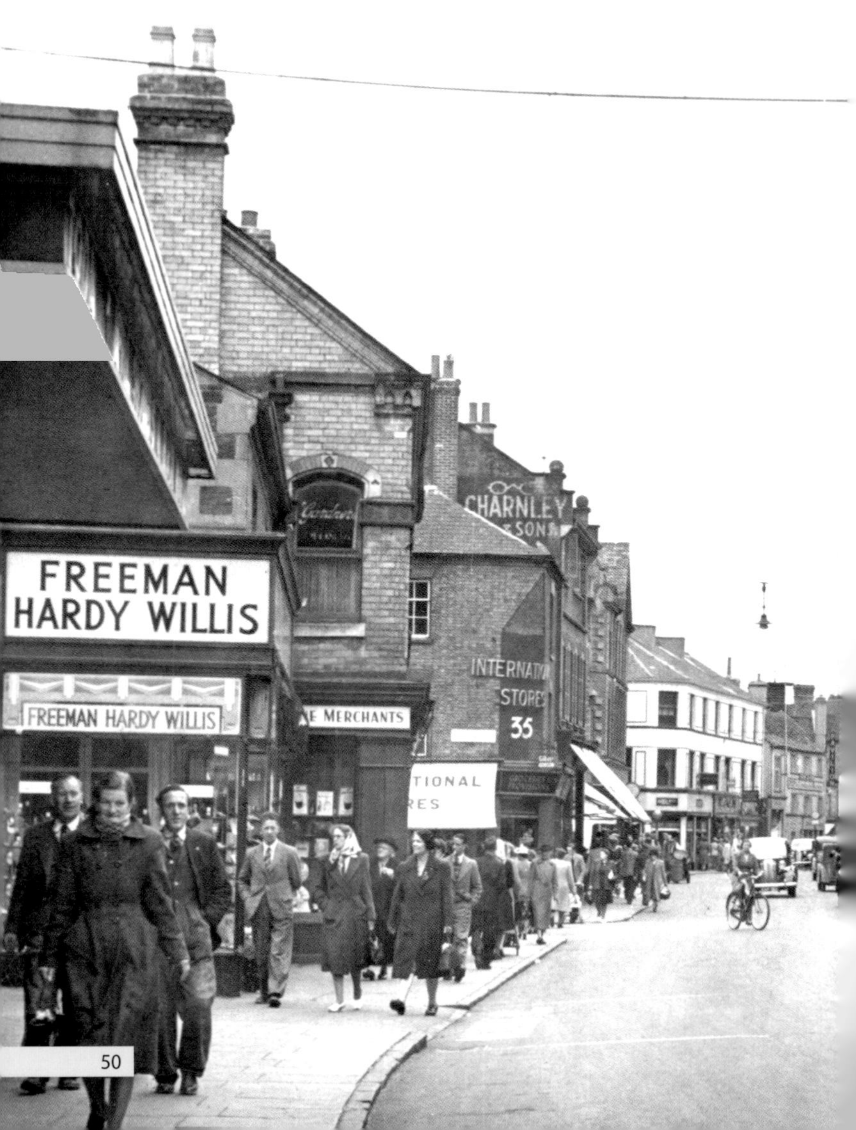

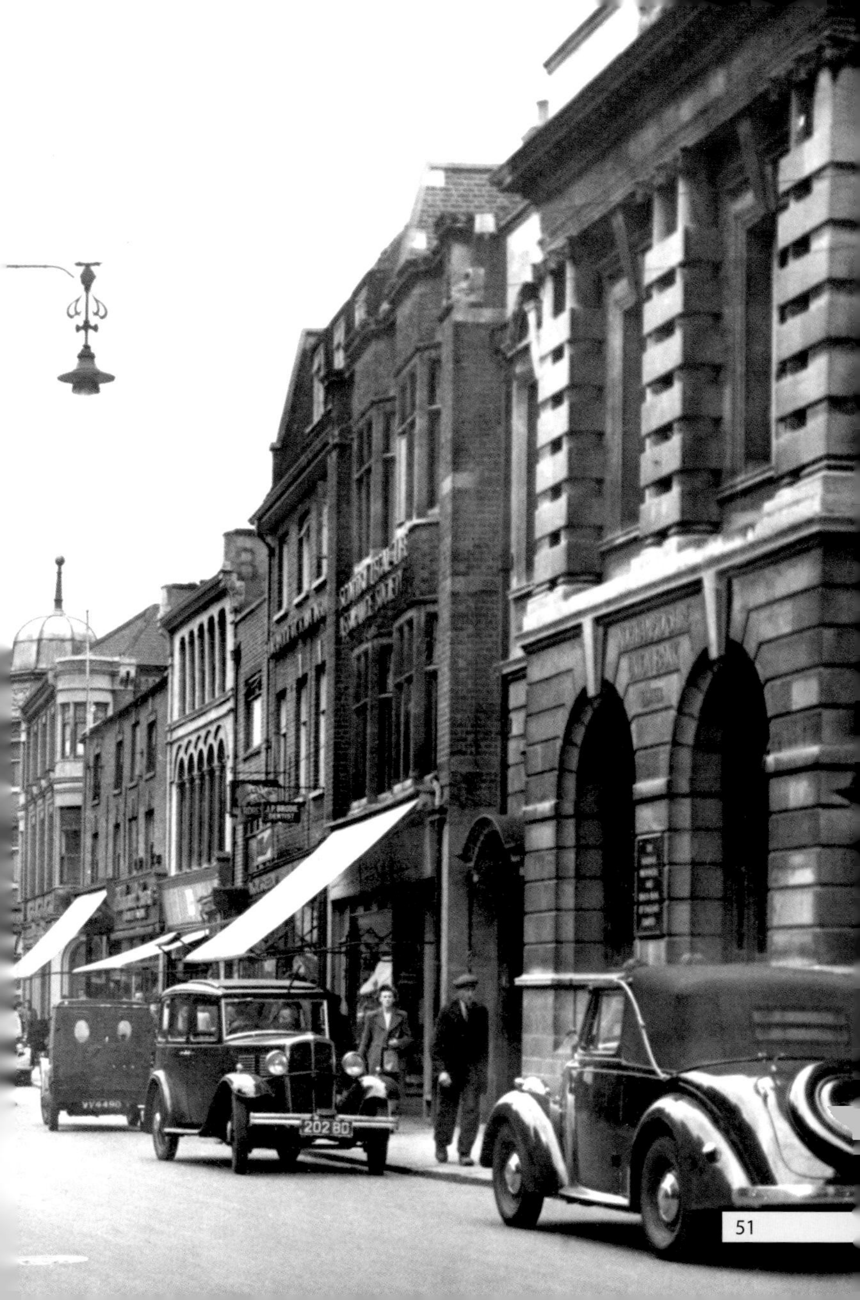

HIGH STREET c1960 K13081

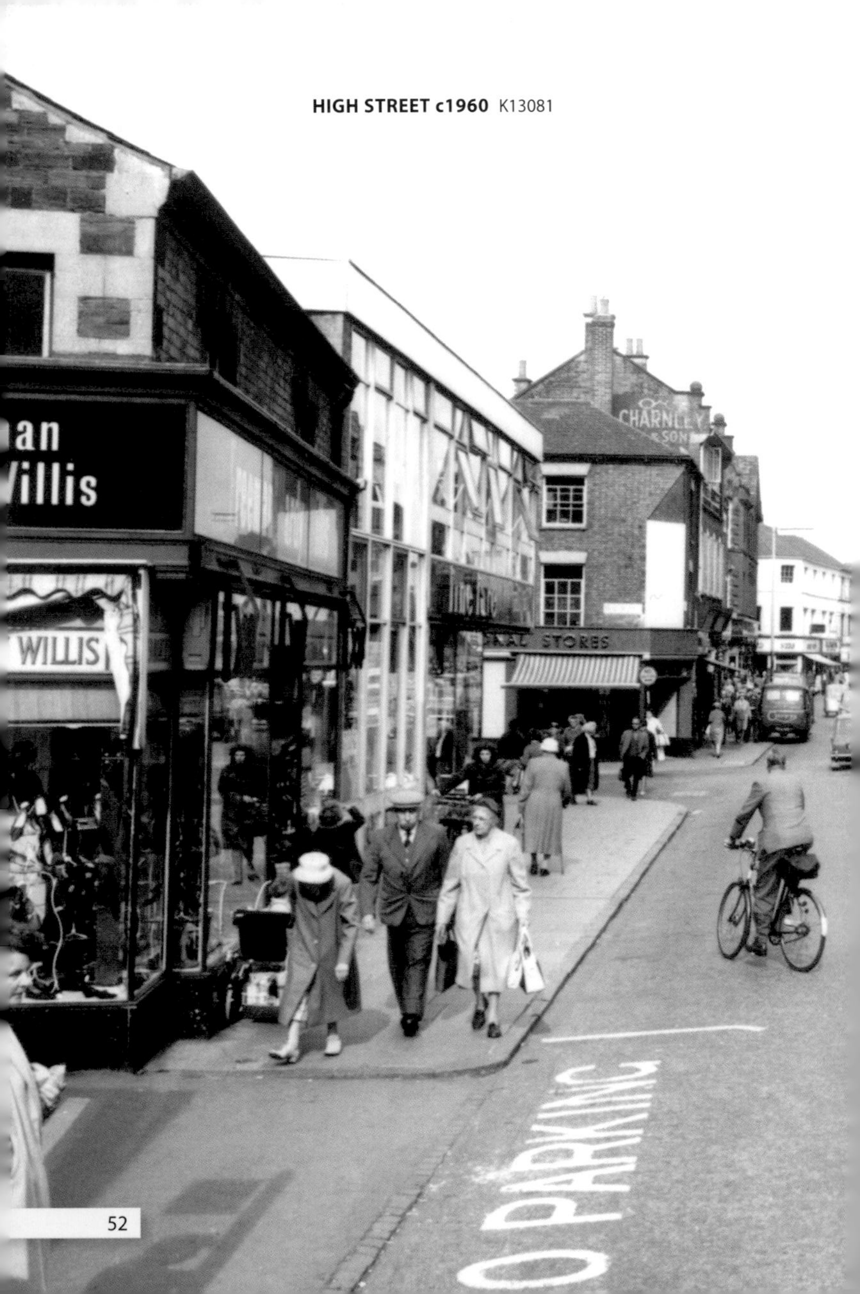

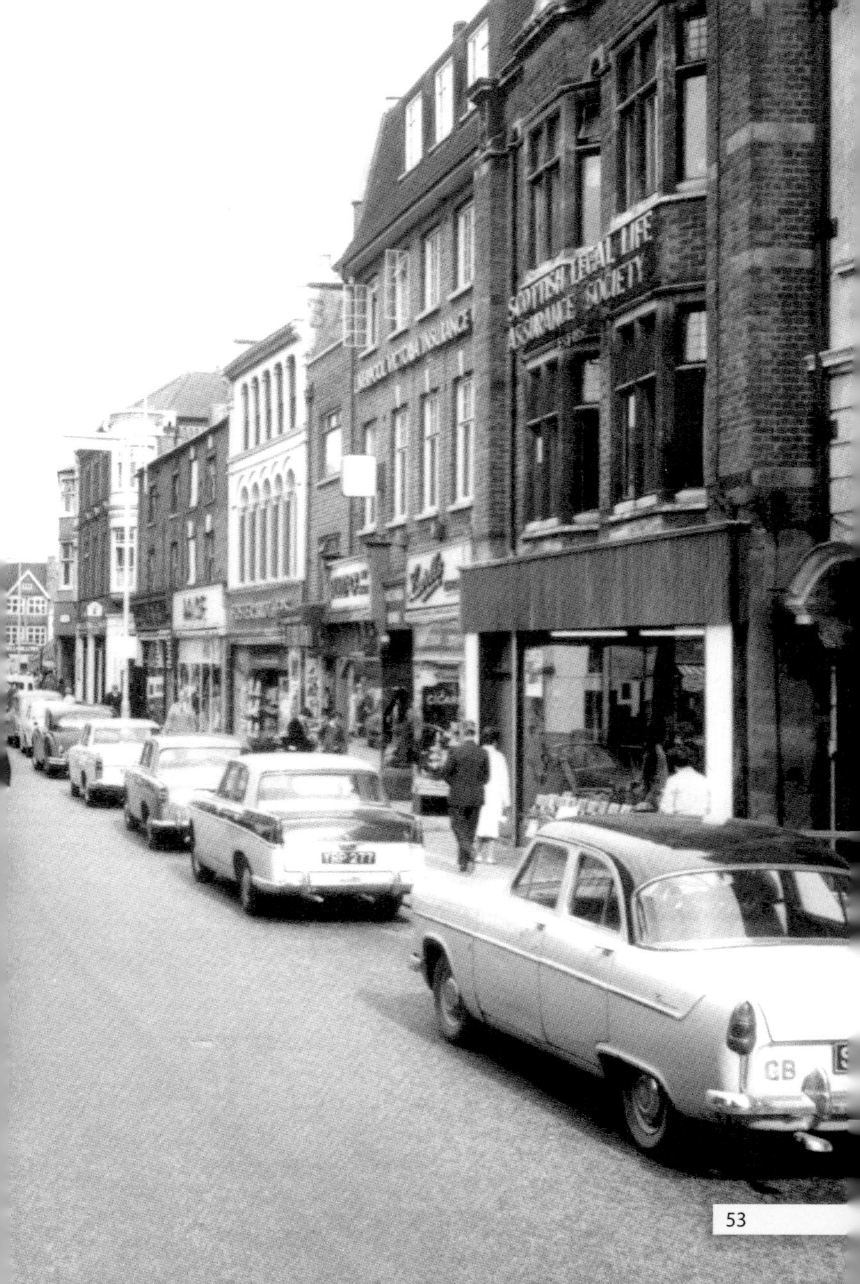
SCOTTISH LEGAL LIFE
ASSURANCE SOCIETY
YRP 277
GB

FRANCIS FRITH

PIONEER VICTORIAN PHOTOGRAPHER

Francis Frith, founder of the world-famous photographic archive, was a complex and multi-talented man. A devout Quaker and a highly successful Victorian businessman, he was philosophical by nature and pioneering in outlook. By 1855 he had already established a wholesale grocery business in Liverpool, and sold it for the astonishing sum of £200,000, which is the equivalent today of over £15,000,000. Now in his thirties, and captivated by the new science of photography, Frith set out on a series of pioneering journeys up the Nile and to the Near East.

INTRIGUE AND EXPLORATION

He was the first photographer to venture beyond the sixth cataract of the Nile. Africa was still the mysterious 'Dark Continent', and Stanley and Livingstone's historic meeting was a decade into the future. The conditions for picture taking confound belief. He laboured for hours in his wicker dark-room in the sweltering heat of the desert, while the volatile chemicals fizzed dangerously in their trays. Back in London he exhibited his photographs and was 'rapturously cheered' by members of the Royal Society. His reputation as a photographer was made overnight.

VENTURE OF A LIFE-TIME

By the 1870s the railways had threaded their way across the country, and Bank Holidays and half-day Saturdays had been made obligatory by Act of Parliament. All of a sudden the working man and his family were able to enjoy days out, take holidays, and see a little more of the world.

With typical business acumen, Francis Frith foresaw that these new tourists would enjoy having souvenirs to commemorate their days out. For the next thirty years he travelled the country by train and by pony and trap, producing fine photographs of seaside resorts and beauty spots that were keenly bought by millions of Victorians. These prints were painstakingly pasted into family albums and pored over during the dark nights of winter, rekindling precious memories of summer excursions. Frith's studio was soon supplying retail shops all over the country, and by 1890 F Frith & Co had become the greatest specialist photographic publishing company in the world, with over 2,000 sales outlets, and pioneered the picture postcard.

FRANCIS FRITH'S LEGACY

Francis Frith had died in 1898 at his villa in Cannes, his great project still growing. By 1970 the archive he created contained over a third of a million pictures showing 7,000 British towns and villages.

Frith's legacy to us today is of immense significance and value, for the magnificent archive of evocative photographs he created provides a unique record of change in the cities, towns and villages throughout Britain over a century and more. Frith and his fellow studio photographers revisited locations many times down the years to update their views, compiling for us an enthralling and colourful pageant of British life and character.

We are fortunate that Frith was dedicated to recording the minutiae of everyday life. For it is this sheer wealth of visual data, the painstaking chronicle of changes in dress, transport, street layouts, buildings, housing and landscape that captivates us so much today, offering us a powerful link with the past and with the lives of our ancestors.

Computers have now made it possible for Frith's many thousands of images to be accessed almost instantly. The archive offers every one of us an opportunity to examine the places where we and our families have lived and worked down the years. Its images, depicting our shared past, are now bringing pleasure and enlightenment to millions around the world a century and more after his death.

For further information visit: www.francisfrith.com

INTERIOR DECORATION

Frith's photographs can be seen framed and as giant wall murals in thousands of pubs, restaurants, hotels, banks, retail stores and other public buildings throughout Britain. These provide interesting and attractive décor, generating strong local interest and acting as a powerful reminder of gentler days in our increasingly busy and frenetic world.

FRITH PRODUCTS

All Frith photographs are available as prints and posters in a variety of different sizes and styles. In the UK we also offer a range of other gift and stationery products illustrated with Frith photographs, although many of these are not available for delivery outside the UK – see our web site for more information on the products available for delivery in your country.

THE INTERNET

Over 100,000 photographs of Britain can be viewed and purchased on the Frith web site. The web site also includes memories and reminiscences contributed by our customers, who have personal knowledge of localities and of the people and properties depicted in Frith photographs. If you wish to learn more about a specific town or village you may find these reminiscences fascinating to browse. Why not add your own comments if you think they would be of interest to others? See **www.francisfrith.com**

PLEASE HELP US BRING FRITH'S PHOTOGRAPHS TO LIFE

Our authors do their best to recount the history of the places they write about. They give insights into how particular towns and villages developed, they describe the architecture of streets and buildings, and they discuss the lives of famous people who lived there. But however knowledgeable our authors are, the story they tell is necessarily incomplete.

Frith's photographs are so much more than plain historical documents. They are living proofs of the flow of human life down the generations. They show real people at real moments in history; and each of those people is the son or daughter of someone, the brother or sister, aunt or uncle, grandfather or grandmother of someone else. All of them lived, worked and played in the streets depicted in Frith's photographs.

We would be grateful if you would give us your insights into the places shown in our photographs: the streets and buildings, the shops, businesses and industries. Post your memories of life in those streets on the Frith website: what it was like growing up there, who ran the local shop and what shopping was like years ago; if your workplace is shown tell us about your working day and what the building is used for now. Read other visitors' memories and reconnect with your shared local history and heritage. With your help more and more Frith photographs can be brought to life, and vital memories preserved for posterity, and for the benefit of historians in the future.

Wherever possible, we will try to include some of your comments in future editions of our books. Moreover, if you spot errors in dates, titles or other facts, please let us know, because our archive records are not always completely accurate—they rely on 140 years of human endeavour and hand-compiled records. You can email us using the contact form on the website.

Thank you!

For further information, trade, or author enquiries
please contact us at the address below:

The Francis Frith Collection, Frith's Barn, Teffont, Salisbury, Wiltshire, England SP3 5QP.

Tel: +44 (0)1722 716 376 Fax: +44 (0)1722 716 881

e-mail: sales@francisfrith.co.uk **www.francisfrith.com**